Fundamental Reappraisal of the Discount Mechanism: Financial Instability Revisited: The Economics of Disaster

Hyman P. Minsky

The BiblioGov Project is an effort to expand awareness of the public documents and records of the U.S. Government via print publications. In broadening the public understanding of government and its work, an enlightened democracy can grow and prosper. Ranging from historic Congressional Bills to the most recent Budget of the United States Government, the BiblioGov Project spans a wealth of government information. These works are now made available through an environmentally friendly, print-on-demand basis, using only what is necessary to meet the required demands of an interested public. We invite you to learn of the records of the U.S. Government, heightening the knowledge and debate that can lead from such publications.

Included are the following Collections:

Budget of The United States Government
Presidential Documents
United States Code
Education Reports from ERIC
GAO Reports
History of Bills
House Rules and Manual
Public and Private Laws

Code of Federal Regulations
Congressional Documents
Economic Indicators
Federal Register
Government Manuals
House Journal
Privacy act Issuances
Statutes at Large

FUNDAMENTAL REAPPRAISAL OF THE DISCOUNT MECHANISM

FINANCIAL INSTABILITY REVISITED: THE ECONOMICS OF DISASTER

HYMAN P. MINSKY

Prepared for the Steering Committee for the Fundamental Reappraisal of the Discount Mechanism Appointed by the Board of Governors of the Federal Reserve System

The following paper is one of a series prepared by the research staffs of the Board of Governors of the Federal Reserve System and of the Federal Reserve Banks and by academic economists in connection with the Fundamental Reappraisal of the Discount Mechanism.

The analyses and conclusions set forth are those of the author and do not necessarily indicate concurrence by other members of the research staffs, by the Board of Governors, or by the Federal Reserve Banks.

FUNDAMENTAL REAPPRAISAL OF THE DISCOUNT MECHANISM

FINANCIAL INSTABILITY REVISITED:

The Economics of Disaster

by

Hyman P. Minsky

Professor of Economics

Washington University

The original draft of this paper was written in the fall of
1966 and it was revised in January 1970. I wish to thank Maurice I.
Townsend, Lawrence H. Seltzer, and Bernard Shull for their comments
and encouragement. Needless to say any errors of fact or fancy are
my responsibility.

TABLE OF CONTENTS

Page

I. Introduction

A striking characteristic of economic experience in the United States is the repeated occurrence of financial crises--crises that usher in deep depressions and periods of low-level economic stagnation. More than 40 years have now passed since the financial shock that initiated the Great Depression of the 1930's, a much longer period of time than between the crises and deep depressions of the previous century.[1/] Is the experience since the Great Depression the result of fundamental changes in the economic system and our knowledge so that crises and deep depressions cannot happen or are the fundamental relations unchanged and our knowledge and power still inadequate so that crises and deep depressions are still possible?

This paper argues that the fundamentals are unchanged; sustained economic growth, business cycle booms, and the accompanying financial developments still generate conditions conducive to disaster for the entire economic system.

Every disaster, financial or otherwise, is compounded out of initial displacements or shocks, structural characteristics of the system, and human error. The theory developed here argues that the structural

---

[1/] For the chronology of mild and deep depression cycles see M. Friedman and A. J. Schwartz, "Money and Business Cycles."

In their chronology of mild and of deep depression, all clearly deep depression cycles were associated with a financial crisis and all clearly mild depression cycles were not. Friedman and Schwartz choose to ignore this phenomena. preferring a monolithic explanation for both 1929-33 and 1960-61 · It seems better to posit that mild and deep depressions are quite different types of beasts and the differences in length and depth are due to the absence or occurrence of a financial panic. See H. P. Minsky, "Comment on Friedman and Schwartz's Money and Business Cycles."

characteristics of the financial system change during periods of prolonged
expansion and economic boom and that these changes cumulate to decrease
the stability of the system. Thus, after an expansion has been in progress
   domain of
for some time, an event that is not of unusual size or duration can trigger
a sharp financial reaction.[2/]

       Displacements may be the result of system behavior or human
error. Once the sharp financial reaction occurs, institutional deficiencies
will be evident. Thus after a crisis it will always be possible to construct
plausible arguments--by emphasizing the triggering events or institutional
flaws--that accidents, mistakes, or easily corrected shortcomings were
responsible for the disaster.[3/]

       In previous work, I have used an accelerator-multiplier cum constrain-
ing ceilings and floors model to represent the real economy. Within this
model the periodic falling away from the ceiling, which reflects parameter
values and hence is an endogenous phenomenon, is the not unusual event that
can trigger the 'unstable' financial reaction--if a 'proper' financial
environment or structure exists. The financial reaction in turn lowers
the affective floor to income. Once the gap between floor and ceiling
incomes is large enough, I assumed that the accelerator coefficient falls
to a value that leads to a stagnant behavior for the economy. In this
way a set of parameter values that leads to an explosive income expansion is

---

2/ I. Fisher, "The Debt Deflation Theory of Great Depressions."

3/ See M. Friedman and A. J. Schwartz, A Monetary History of the United
States 1867-1960,   pp. 309 and 310, footnote 9, for a rather startling
example of such reasoning.

replaced by a set that leads to a stagnant economy. I assumed that the gap between floor and ceiling income is a determinant of the accelerator coefficient and that the immediate impact of financial instability is to lower the floor income, because financial variables--including the market value of common stocks--determine the position of a conventional Keynesian consumption function.[4/]

This view neglects decision-making under uncertainty as a determinant of system behavior. A special type of uncertainty is inherent in an enterprise system with decentralized decisions and private ownership of productive resources due to the financial relations. The financial system of such an economy partitions and distributes uncertainty. A model that recognizes the problems involved in decision-making in the face of the intrinsically irrational fact of uncertainty is needed if financial instability is to be understood. A reinterpretation of Keynesian economics as just such a model, and an examination of how monetary constraint (whether due to policy or to behavior of the economy) works, are needed before the stability properties of the financial system and thus of the economy can be examined. It turns out that the fundamental instability of a capitalist economy is a tendency to explode--to enter into a boom or "euphoric" state.

This paper will not present any empirical research. There is, nevertheless, need to: (1) examine updated information of the type analyzed in earlier studies, (2) explore additional bodies of data, and (3) generate new data (see Section VII). Only with this information can the problem be made precise and the propositions tested.

4/ H. P. Minsky, "Financial Crisis, Financial Systems, and the Performance of the Economy."

H. P. Minsky, "A Linear Model of Cyclical Growth."

There is a special facet to empirical work on the problems at
issue. Financial crises, panics, and instability are rare events with
short durations.[5] We have not experienced anything more than unit or
minor sectoral financial distress since the early 1930's. The institutions
and usages in finance, due to both legislation and the evolution of financial practices, are much different today from what they were before the
Great Depression. For example, it is necessary to "guess" the power of
deposit insurance in order to estimate the conditions under which a crisis
can develop from a set of initial events.[6] The short durations of crises
means that the smoothing operations that go into data generations as well
as econometric analysis will tend to minimize the importance of crises.

Because of such factors it might be that the most meaningful
way to test propositions as to the cause and effect of financial
instability will be through simulation studies, where the simulation models
are designed to reflect alternative ways that financial instability can
be induced.[7]

In this paper, Section II discusses differences between an
economy that is simply growing steadily and one that is booming. The
characteristics of an euphoric economy are identified. This section develops
the proposition that, in a boom or euphoric economy, the willingness to

[5] The large and long contraction of 1929-33 can be interpreted as a
succession of crises compounding an initial disturbance.

[6] Perhaps the financial history of 1966 can be interpreted as a test of
the power of deposit insurance to offset the destabilizing aspects of
financial constraint.

[7] H. P. Minsky, "Financial Crisis, Financial Systems, and the Performance
of the Economy," pp. 326-70, where a number of 'primitive' simulations
are presented.

invest and to emit liabilities is such that demand conditions will lead to tight money markets--defined in terms of the level and rate of change of interest rates and other financing terms--independently of the rate of growth of the money supply.

Section III focuses upon cash flows due to income production, balance sheet relations and transactions in real and financial assets. The likelihood of financial instability occurring is dependent upon the relationship between cash payment commitments and the normal sources of cash, as well as upon the behavior of markets that will be affected if unusual sources for cash need to be tapped.

Section IV develops the role of uncertainty as a determinant of the demand for investment within a Keynesian framework.

Section V examines alternative modes of operation of monetary constraint. In a euphoric economy, tight money, when effective, does not operate by inducing a smooth movement along a stable investment schedule; rather it operates by shifting the liquidity preference function. Such shifts are typically due to a 'liquidity crisis' of some sort.

Section VI explores the domains of stability both of the financial system and of the economy. These domains are shown to be endogenous and to decrease during a prolonged boom. In addition, the financial changes that take place during a euphoric period tend also to decrease the domain of stability and the feedbacks from euphoria tend to induce sectoral financial difficulties that can escalate to a general financial panic. If such a panic occurs, it will usher in a deep depression; however, the central bank can abort a financial crisis. Nevertheless the tensions and tremors that pass through the financial system during such a period of near crisis may lead to a reconsideration of desired portfolio composition by both financial institutions and other economic units. A rather severe recession may follow such a reconsideration.

Sections VII and VIII deal with two special topics, bank examinations and regional impacts. In Section VII it is argued that a bank examination procedure centering around cash flows as determined by balance sheet and contractual relations, would be a valuable guide for Federal Reserve policy and an important instrument for bank management. Such an examination procedure would force managers of financial units and economic policy-makers to consider the impact upon financial units of the characteristics of both the real economy and the financial system.

The discussion of the regional impact of Section VIII centers around the possibility that there is a concentration of financially vulnerable units within one region. In these circumstances the escalation of financial constraint to a financial crisis might occur though financially vulnerable units, on a national basis, are too few to cause difficulty.

Section sets forth some policy guidelines for the Federal Reserve System. It is argued that the discount window should be open to selected money market position takers (dealers) and that the Federal Reserve should move toward furnishing a larger portion of the total reserves of banks by discounting operations. This policy strategy follows from the increased awareness of the possibility of a financial crisis and of the need to have "broad, deep, and resilient markets" for a wide spectrum of financial instruments once a financial crisis threatens in order to moderate its effects.

II. The Economics of Euphoria

In the mid-1960's the U.S. economy experienced a "change of state." Political leaders and official economists announced that the economic system had entered upon a new era that was to be characterized by the end of the business cycle as it had been known.[8] From then on, cycles, if any, would be in the positive rate of growth of income. The doctrine of "fine tuning" went further and asserted that even recessions in the rate of growth of income could be avoided. Contemporary business comments were consistent with these official views.

The substance of the change of state was an investment boom: in each year from 1963 through 1966 the rate of increase of investment by corporate business rose.[9] By the mid-1960's business investment was guided by a belief that the future promised perpetual expansion. An economy that is ruled by such expectations and that exhibits such investment behavior can properly be labeled euphoric.

Consider the value of a going concern. Expected gross profits after taxes reflect the expected behavior of the economy, as well as expected market and management developments. Two immediate consequences follow, if the expectation of a normal business cycle is replaced by the

---

8/ J. Tobin, The Intellectual Revolution in U.S. Economic Policy Making.

9/ Investment-Nonfarm, nonfinancial corporations, 1962-66:

Year	Purchase of physical assets	
	Billions of dollars	Growth rate (per cent)
1962	44.7	--
1963	76.7	4.5
1964	53.5	14.6
1965	64.9	21.3
1966	79.8	21.6[*]

Source: Economic Report of the President, 1969, Table B73.

* The 'Crunch' of 1966 occurred in late August/early September; this put a damper on investment and the purchase of physical assets declined to $74.1 billion in 1967.

expectation of steady growth. First, those gross profits in the present value calculations that had reflected expected "recessions" are replaced by those that reflect continuing expansion. Simultaneously there is less uncertainty about the future behavior of the economy. As the belief in the reality of a new era emerges, the decrease in the expected down or short time for plant and equipment raises their present values. The confident expectation of a steady stream of prosperity gross profits makes portfolio plunging more appealing to firm decision makers.

A sharp rise in expected returns from real capital makes the economy short of capital overnight. The willingness to assume liability structures that are less defensive and to take, what would have been considered in earlier times undesirable, chances in order to finance the acquisition of additional capital goods means that this shortage of capital will be transformed into demand for financial resources.

Those that supply financial resources live in the same expectational climate as those that demand them. In the several financial markets, once a change in expectations occurs, demanders, with liability structures that would in the view of the suppliers have made them ineligible previously for accommodations, become quite acceptable. Thus the supply conditions for financing the acquisitions of real capital improve simultaneously with an increase in the willingness to emit liabilities to finance such acquisitions.

A new era is destabilizing, in an expansionary direction, in three senses. One is that it quite rapidly raises the value of existing capital. The second is an increase in the willingness to finance the acquisition of real capital by emitting what, previously, would have been considered as high-cost liabilities, where the cost of liabilities includes risk or uncertainty borne by the liability emitter (borrower's risk). The third is the acceptance by lenders of assets that previously would have been considered as low-yield--when the yield is adjusted to allow for the risks borne by the asset acquirer (lender's risk).[10]

These concepts can be made more precise. The present value of a set of capital goods collected in a firm reflects that firm's expected gross profits after taxes. For all enterprises there is a pattern of how the business cycles of history have affected their gross profits. Initially the present value reflects this past cyclical pattern. For example, with a short horizon

$$V = \frac{Q_1}{1 + r_1} + \frac{Q_2}{(1 + r_2)^2} + \frac{Q_3}{(1 + r_3)^3}$$

where Q_1 is a prosperity, Q_2 is a recession, and Q_3 is a recovery gross profits after taxes, $(Q_2 < Q_3 < Q_1)$. With the new era expectations Q_2' and Q_3', prosperity returns replace the depression and recovery returns. As a result we have: V(new era) > V (traditional). This rise in the value of extant capital assets as collected in firms increases the prices that firms are willing to pay for additions to their capital assets.

Generally, the willingness to emit liabilities is constrained by the need to hedge or protect the organization against the occurrence of un-favorable conditions. Let us call Q_2'' and Q_3'' the gross profits after taxes if a possible, but not really expected, deep and long recession occurs. As a risk averter the portfolio rule might be that the balance-sheet

---

11/ M. Kalecki, "The Principle of Increasing Risk."

structure must be such that even if Q_2" and Q_3" do occur no$_\wedge$consequences [serious] will follow; Q_2" and Q_3"--though not likely--are significant determinants of desired balance-sheet structure.[11/] As a result if the euphoric change in "state," the view grows that Q_2" and Q_3" are so unlikely that there is no need to protect the organization against them. A liability structure that was expensive in terms of risk now becomes cheap when there were significant chances of Q_2" and Q_3" occurring. The cost of capital or of finance by way of such liability structures decreases.

Financial institutions are simultaneously demanders in one and suppliers in another set of financial market. Once euphoria sets in, they accept liability structures—their own and those of borrowers--that, in a more sober expectational climate, they would have rejected. Money and Treasury bills become poor assets to hold with the decline in the uncertainty Discount on assets whose returns depend upon the performance of the economy. The shift to euphoria increases the willingness of financial institutions to acquire assets by engaging in liquidity-decreasing portfolio transformations.

A euphoric new era means that an investment boom is combined with pervasive liquidity-decreasing portfolio transformation. Money market interest rates rise because the demand for investment is increasing, and the elasticity of this demand decreases with respect to market interest rates and contractural terms. In a complex financial system, it is possible to finance investment by portfolio transformations. Thus when a euphoric transformation of expectations takes place, in the short run the amount of investment financed can be independent of monetary policy. The desire to expand and the willingness to finance expansion by portfolio

---

11/ W. Fellner, "Average Cost Pricing and the Theory of Uncertainty."

Feller, "Monetary Policies and Hoarding in Periods of Stagnation."

S. A. Ozga, Expectations in Economic Theory.

changes can be so great that, unless these are serious side effects of
feedbacks, an inflationary explosion becomes likely.

A euphoric boom economy is affected by the financial heritage
of an earlier more insecure time. The world is not born anew each moment.
Past portfolio decisions and conditions in financial markets are embodied
in the stock of financial instruments. In particular a decrease in the
market value of assets which embody protections against states of nature
that are now considered unlikely to occur will take place or alternatively
there is a rise in the interest rate that must be paid to induce portfolios
to hold newly created assets with these characteristics. To the extent
that such assets are long lived and held by deposit institutions with short-
term or demand liabilities, pressures upon these deposit institutions will
accompany the euphoric state of the economy. In addition the same
change of state that led to the investment boom and to the increased willingness to emit debt affects the portfolio preferences of the holders of the
liabilities of deposit institutions. These institutions must meet interest
rate competition at a time when the market value of the safety they sell
has decreased; that is, their interest rates must rise by more than other
rates.

The rising interest rate on safe assets during an euphoric boom
puts strong pressures on financial institutions that offer protection and
safety. The linkages between these deposit institutions--conventions as
to financing arrangements and particular real markets--are such that
sectoral depressive pressures are fed back from a boom to particular markets;
these depressive pressures are part of the mechanism by which real resources
are shifted.

The rise in interest rates places serious pressures upon particular financial intermediaries. In the current (1966) era the saving and loan associations and the mutual savings banks, together with the closely related homebuilding industry, seem to take a large part of the initial feedback pressure. It may be that additional feedback pressures are on life insurance and consumer finance companies.

A little understood facet of how financial and real values are linked centers around the effect of stock market values.[12] The value of real capital rises when the expectation that a recession will occur diminishes and this rise will be reflected in equity prices. The increased ratio of debt financing can also raise expected returns on equities. Inasmuch as owners of wealth live in the same expectational climate as corporate officers, portfolio preferences shift toward equities as the belief in the possibility of a recession or depression diminishes. Thus a stock market boom feeds upon and feeds an investment boom.

The financing needs of the investment boom raises interest rates. This rise lowers the market value of long-term debt and adversely affects some financial institutions. Higher interest rates also increase the cost of credit used to finance positions in equities. Initially the competition for funds among various financial sectors facilitates the rapid expansion of the economy; then as interest rates rise, it constrains the profits of investing units and makes the carrying of equities more expensive. This first tends to decrease the rate of increase of equity prices and then to lower equity prices.

---

[12] R. Turvey, "Does the Rate of Interest Rule the Roost."

J. M. Keynes, The General Theory of Employment, Interest and Money. New York, 1936. Chapter XII.

All in all the euphoric period has a short life span. Local and sectoral depressions and the fall in equity prices initiate doubts as to whether a new era really has been achieved. A hedging of portfolios and a reconsideration of investment programs take place. However, the portfolio commitments of the short euphoric era are fixed in liability structures. The reconsideration of investment programs, the lagged effects upon other sectors from the resource shifting pressures, and the inelasticity of aggregate supply which leads to increases in costs combine to yield a shortfall of the income of investing units below the more optimistic of the euphoric expectations.

The result is a combination of cash flow commitments inherited from the burst of euphoria and of cash flow receipts based upon lower-than-expected income. Whether the now less desirable financial positions will be unwound without generating significant shocks or whether a series of financial shocks will occur is not known. In either case, investment demand decreases from its euphoric levels. If the boom is unwound with little trouble, it becomes quite easy for the economy once again to enter a "new era"; on the other hand, if the unwinding involves financial instability, then there are prospects of deep depressions and stagnation.

The pertinent aspects of a euphoric period can be characterized as follows:

1. The tight money of the euphoric period is due more to runaway demand than to constraint upon supply. Thus those who weigh money supply heavily in estimating money market conditions will be misled.

2. The run-up of short- and long-term interest rates places
pressure on deposit savings intermediaries and disrupts industries whose
financial channels run through these intermediaries. There is a feedback
from euphoria to a constrained real demand in some sectors.

3. An essential aspect of a euphoric economy is the construction
of liability structures which imply payments that are closely articulated
directly, or indirectly via layerings, to cash flows due to income production. If the impact of the disruption of financing channels occurs after
a significant build-up of tight financial positions, a further
depressive factor becomes effective.

III. Cash Flows

Financial crises take place because units need or desire more cash than is available from their usual sources and so they resort to unusual ways to raise cash. Various types of cash flows are identified in this section, and the relations among them as well as between cash flows and other characteristics of the economy are examined.

The varying reliability of sources of cash is a well-known phenomenon in banking theory. For a unit, a source of cash may be reliable as long as there is no net market demand for cash upon it, and unreliable whenever there is such net demand upon the source. Under pressure various financial and nonfinancial units may withdraw, either by necessity or because of a defensive financial policy, from some financial markets. Such withdrawals not only affect the potential variability of prices in the market but also may disrupt business connections. Both the ordinary way of doing business and standby and defensive sources of cash can be affected.

Withdrawals on the supply side of financial markets may force demanding units that were under no special strain and were not directly affected by financial stringencies to look for new financing connections. An initial disturbance can cumulate through such third party or innocent bystander impacts. Financial market events that disrupt well-established financing channels affect the present value and cash flows of units not directly affected.[13]

13/ Thus the disruption of the Southern California savings and loan mortgage markets in mid-1966 affected all present values and cash flow expectations in the economy.

For most consumers and nonfinancial (ordinary) business firms the largest source of cash results from their current income. Wages and salaries are the major source of cash to most consumers and sales of output are the major source for business firms. For financial intermediaries other than dealers, the ordinary cash flow to the unit can be derived from its financial assets. For example, short-term business debts in a commercial bank's portfolio state the reserve money that borrowers are committed to make available to the bank at the contract dates. A mortgage in a savings and loan association's portfolio states the contractual "cash flow to" for various dates. For financial market dealers cash receipts usually result from the selling out of their position, rather than from the commitments as stated in their inventory of assets. Under ordinary circumstances dealers as going concerns do not expect to sell out their positions, as they sell one set of assets they acquire a new set.

The ordinary sources of cash for various classes of economic units will be called cash flow from operations. All three types of cash flow from operations described above income, financial contracts, and turnover of inventory can be considered as functions of national income. The ability to meet payment commitments depends upon the normal functioning of the income production system.

In addition to cash flow from the sale of assets, dealers-- and other financial and nonfinancial units--can meet cash drains due to the need to make payments on liabilities by emitting new liabilities. This second source of cash is called the refinancing of positions.

Furthermore, liquidating, or running off, a position is the
third possible way for some units to obtain cash. This is what retailers
and wholesalers do when they sell inventories (seasonal retailers actually
do liquidate by selling out their position in, say, Christmas toys).

The financial assets and the liabilities of an economic unit can
be transformed into time series of contractual cash receipts and payments.
The various items in these contractual receipts and payments depend upon
national income: the fulfillment of the terms of mortgage contracts
depends upon consumer disposable income and so forth.[14] Estimates of
the direct and indirect impact of variations in national income upon the
ability of units in various sectors to meet financial commitments can be
derived.[15]

Each economic unit has its reserve, or emergency, sources
of cash. For many units the emergency source consists of positions
in some marketable or redeemable assets. Savings bonds and time deposits
are typical standby sources of cash for consumers. A corporation may keep
a reserve in Treasury bills or other money market instruments to meet either
unusual needs for cash or an unexpected shortfall in cash receipts.
Hoards of idle cash serve this purpose for all units. Cash has the special
virtue that its availability does not depend upon the normal functioning
of any market.

In principle the normal and secondary sources of cash for all
units can be identified and their ratio to financial commitments can be

14/ This becomes the 'rationale' for a cash flow bank examination. The
deviation of actual from contractual cash flows depends upon the behavior
of the economy.

15/ The Minsky-Bonen experiments in H. P. Minsky, "Financial Crisis,
Financial Systems, and the Performance of the Economy," were primitive
attempts to do this.

estimated. By far the largest number of units use their income receipts to meet their financial commitments. Mortgage and consumer instalment payments for consumers and interest and sinking fund payments for businesses would be financed normally by income cash flows.

The substitution of a deposit by customer B for a deposit from customer A in a bank liability structure may be viewed as the refinancing of a position. The typical financial unit acquires cash to meet its payment commitments, as stated in its liabilities, not from any cash flow from its assets or by selling assets but rather by emitting substitute liabilities. (The only financial organizations that seem to use cash flows from assets to meet cash flow commitments are the closed-end investment trusts, both levered and unlevered.)

When a unit which normally meets its financial commitments by drawing upon an income cash flow finds it necessary, or desirable, to refinance its position, additional pressures may be placed upon financial institutions.

Some financial relations are based upon the periodic liquidation of positions--for example, the seasonal inventory in retailing. Capital market dealers or underwriters liquidate positions in one set of assets in order to acquire new assets. However if organizations that normally finance their payments by using cash from either income or refinancing of positions should instead attempt to sell their positions, it may turn out that the market for the assets in position is thin: as a result a sharp fall in the price of the asset occurs with a small increase in supply. In the market for single-family homes a sale is usually not a forced sale, and to a large extent sellers of one house are buyers or renters

of another. If homeowners as a class tried to sell out their houses,
the market would not be able to handle this without significant price
concessions. But significant price concessions mean a decline in net
worth--not only for the selling unit but for all units holding this asset.
More particularly a fall in price may mean that the offering units
may be unable to raise the required or expected cash by dealing in the
affected asset.

As an empirical generalization, almost all financial commitments
are met from two normal sources of cash: income flows and refinancing of
positions. For most units--especially those which have real capital goods
as their asset--the selling out of their position is not feasible [no market
exists for a quick sale] for others, aside from marginal adjustments
by way of special money markets, it is an unusual source of cash.

A further empirical generalization is that asset prices--prices
of the stock--can fall much more rapidly than income prices--prices of the
flow.[16] Any need or desire to acquire cash that leads to attempts to sell
out positions in reproducible assets will result not only in large-scale
decreases in net worth but also in market prices for reproducible assets
that are far below their current cost of production.

Even in the face of a widespread need or desire to acquire cash
by selling assets, not all assets are allowed to fall in price. The price
of some assets will be stabilized by central bank purchases or loans
(refinancing positions); such assets can be called protected assets.

16/ This is the content of the alleged wage rigidity assumption of Keynesian
theory. See H. G. Johnson, "The 'General Theory' after Twenty Five Years."

Financial instability occurs whenever a large number of units resort to extraordinary sources for cash. The conditions under which extraordinary sources of cash have to be tapped--which for financial units means mainly that the conditions in which positions have to be liquidated (run off or sold out)--are the conditions that can trigger financial instability. The adequacy of cash flows from income relative to debt , the adequacy of refinancing possibilities relative to position, and the ratio of unprotected to protected financial assets are determinants of the stability of the financial system. The trend or evolution of the likelihood of financial instability depends upon the trend or evolution of the determinants of financial stability.

IV. Financial Instability and Income Determination

The essential difference between Keynesian and both classical and neoclassical economics is the importance attached to uncertainty.[17] Basic propositions in classical and neoclassical economics are derived by abstracting from uncertainty; the most that uncertainty does is add some minor qualifications to the propositions of the theory. The special Keynesian propositions with respect to money, investment, and underemployment equilibrium, as well as the treatment of consumption, can be understood only as statements about system behavior in a world with uncertainty. One defense against some possible highly undesirable consequences of some possible states of the world is to make appropriate defensive portfolio choices.[18]

---

[17] I include the conventional interpretation of Keynes under the ruberic of neoclassical economics. This standard interpretation, which "took off" from Hicks' famous article, "Mr. Keynes and the 'Classics,' A Suggested Interpretation," and which since has been entombed in standard works like G. Ackley, Macroeconomic Theory, is inconsistent with Keynes' own succinct and clear statement of the content of the general theory in his rebuttal to Viner's famous review ("Mr. Keynes on the Causes of Employment.") Keynes' rebuttal appeared with the title "The General Theory of Employment," and emphasized the dominance of uncertainty in the determination of portfolios, the pricing of capital, and the pace of investment.

[18] J. K. Galbraith in The Affluent Society and K. J. Arrow, "Uncertainty and the Welfare Economics of Medical Care," take the view that various labor and product market deviations from competitive conditions reflect the need to constrain the likelihood that undesirable "states" of the world will occur. This Galbraith-Arrow view of the optimal behavior of firms and households seems to complement the view in Keynes' rebuttal to Viner. See also K. J. Arrow, Aspects of the Theory of Risk Bearing, Lecture 2: "The Theory of Risk Aversion," and Lecture 3: "Insurance, Risk and Resource Allocation."

In an attempt to make precise his view of the nature of uncertainty and what his "General Theory" was all about, Keynes asserted that in a world without uncertainty, no one, outside a lunatic asylum, would use money as a store of wealth.[19] In the world as it is, money and Treasury bills are held as assets. Portfolios reflect the choices that sane men make as they attempt to behave in a rational manner in an inherently irrational (unpredictable) universe. This means that a significant proportion of wealth holders try to arrange their portfolios so that they are reasonably well protected irrespective of which of a number of alternative possible states of the economy actually occurs.

In making portfolio choices, economic units do not accept any one thing as a proven guide to the future state of the economy. Unless there are strong reasons for doing otherwise, they often are guided by extrapolation of the current situation or trend, even though they may have doubts about its reliability.[20] Because of this underlying lack of confidence, expectations and hence present values of future incomes are

---

[19] J. M. Keynes, "The General Theory of Employment," *Quarterly Journal of Economics*, pp. 209-23. The exact quotation, in full, is: "Money, it is well known, serves two principal purposes. By acting as a money of account it facilitates exchange without it being necessary that it should ever come into the picture as a substantive object. In this respect it is a convenience which is devoid of significance or real influence. In the second place it is a store of wealth. So we are told without a smile on the face. But in the world of the classical economy, what an insane use to which to put it! For it is a recognized characteristic of money as a store of wealth that it is barren; whereas practically every other form of storing wealth yields some interest or profit. Why should anyone outside a lunatic asylum wish to use money as a store of wealth?" p. 215.

[20] The doubts can take the form of uncertainty as to what 'inertia' should be attached; should it be attached to the level, the rate of change (velocity) or the rate of change of the rate of change (acceleration)?

inherently unstable; thus a not unusual event, such as a 'salad oil scandal' or a modest decline in income, if it occurs in a favorable environment, can lead to a sharp revaluation of expectations and thus of asset values. It may lead not only to a sharp change in what some particular rational man expects but also to a marked change in the consenses as to the future of the economy.

Conceptually the process of setting a value upon a particular long-term asset or a collection of such assets can be separated into two stages. In the first the subjective beliefs about the likelihood of alternative states of the economy in successive time periods are assumed to be held with confidence. A second stage assesses the degree of "belief" in the stated likelihoods attached to the various alternatives.

When beliefs about the actual occurrence of various alternative states of the economy are held with perfect confidence, the standard probability expected value calculation make sense. The present value of a long- term asset reflects its (subjective) expected yield at each state-date of the economy and the assumed likelihood of these state-dates occurring. Under stable conditions, the expected gross profit after taxes (cash flow) of the ith asset at the tth date, Q_{it}, will equal $\Sigma\, p_{st} Q_{si}$ where Q_{si} is the gross profit after taxes of the ith asset if the sth state of nature occurs (assumed independent of date, could be modified to s_{it}, the ith state of nature at the $t^{\underline{th}}$ date) and p_{st} is the (subjective) probability that the sth state will occur at the tth date. The s states are so defined that for each t, $\Sigma\, p_{st} = 1$. These Q_{it}, discounted at a rate appropriate to

the assumed perfect certainty with which the expectations are held, yields
the present value of the ith asset, V_i.[21]

Assume that S is a set of mutually exclusive and exhaustive states
of nature. At date t, one of the S, s_j will occur; the $\Sigma p_{sj}=1$. However,
the probabilities, p_{sj}, which must be attached to the alternative outcomes
in order to compute the expected gross profit and the cash flow for date t,
can be accepted with varying degrees of rational belief. The value of the
i^{th} asset will vary, not only with the expected payoffs at various state-
dates of nature and the probabilities attached to these payoffs, but also
with the confidence placed in the probabilities attached to the occurrence
of these various state-dates of nature. That is, $Q_{it} = \phi (\Sigma p_{st} Q_{si})$ where
$0 \leq \phi \leq 1$ and ϕ reflects the confidence with which the particular weights
are attached to the likelihood of various states of nature occurring.

In other words, there are at least two conjectural elements
in determining the expected payoffs, Q_{it} and hence V_{it}: one is that the
Q_{si} are conjectures; the other that the probability distribution of possible
states of nature, as reflected in the p_s, is not known with certainty.

21/ If it is wished, to each outcome Q_{it} a utility $U(Q_{it})$ can be attached.
The probability and present value computation can be undertaken with
respect to utilities. The risk aversion character of a decision unit is
represented by the curvature of the utility function. A change in
confidence can be depicted by a change in curvature, decreased confidence
being indicated by an increase in curvature. If preference systems can
be assumed to reflect experience, then a long period without a deep
depression will decrease the curvature and the occurrence of a financial
crisis will increase the curvature of the preference system. The
psychology of uncertainty and the social psychology of waves of optimism
and pessimism are two points at which economists need guidance from the
relevant sister social sciences. Throughout any discussion of uncertainty
and of economic policy in the framework of uncertainty psychological
assumptions must be made. At times the conclusions depend in a critical
manner upon the psychological assumptions.

Obviously events that affect the confidence placed in any assumed
probability distribution of the possible alternative states may
also affect the confidence placed in the assumed expected payoff if state
s occurs, Q_{si}. A computed present value of any asset V_i may be accepted
with a wide range of confidence--from near certainty to a most tenuous
conjecture. This degree of acceptance affects the market price of the
asset.

The relevant portfolio decisions for consumers, firms, and financial concerns are not made with respect to individual assets, rather they
are made with respect to bundles of assets. The problem of choosing
a portfolio is to combine assets whose payoffs will vary quite independently
as the states of nature vary in order to achieve the unit's objective; which
for a risk averter might be a minimal satisfactory state in any circumstance.
This might be stated as follows: a portfolio is chosen so as to maximize
V given a specified valuation procedure subject to the constraint that $V_s >$
V for every likely state of nature.[22]

The assets available are both inside and outside assets: the
outside assets consist of money and Government debt.[23] The nominal
value of a monetary asset (money plus Government debt) is independent of
the state of the economy. Government debt can exhibit variability in its
nominal value due to interest rate variations, but in conditions where
business cycles occur, its nominal value is not highly correlated with
the expected nominal value of inside assets.

---

[22] Alternatively the desired portfolio objective can be stated in terms of
cash flows; this less conventional view is examined later in Section VI.

[23] J. G. Gurley, and E. Shaw, Money in a Theory of Finance.

We assume that two types of periods can be distinguished: one in which beliefs are held with confidence concerning the likelihood of alternative states of nature occurring within some horizon period and the second in which such beliefs are most insecure. In the second situation "bets" are placed under duress. During these second periods--when what can be called higher order uncertainty rules--markedly lower relative values are attached to assets whose nominal value depends upon the economy's performance. Periods of higher order uncertainty will see portfolios shift toward assets that offer protection against large declines in nominal values. Even though flexibility is almost always a virtue, the premium on assets that permit flexibility will be larger in such periods of higher order uncertainty. For many questions a rational man has the option of saying "I don't know" and of postponing a decision. As a wealth owner he must assess the worth of various assets even when conditions are so fluid that he would rather not make a decision.

Keynesian liquidity preference encompasses both confidence conditions. Expectations as to the likelihood of different states of nature may be held with varying degrees of confidence. During periods of stable expectations, portfolios are managed so that the outcome will be tolerable regardless which state of nature rules. Most units tend to weigh heavily the avoidance of disasters, such as a liquidity crisis for the unit. Assets that offer protection against a liquidity crisis or temporarily disorganized asset markets would be part of a rational portfolio under all circumstances. In addition a preferred market may exist for assets that obviate against capital losses. Thus liquidity preference is defined as a rational person's demand for money as an asset; this leads to a determinate demand function for money for any 'value' of higher order uncertainty.[24]

In addition to periods where the likelihood of various states of nature appear stable, there are troubled periods when the subjective estimates as to the likelihood of various states of nature are held with much less confidence. The risk averter reaction to a decline in confidence is to attempt to increase the weight of assets that yield flexibility in portfolio choices, in other words, to increase the value not only of money but also of all assets that have broad, deep, and resilient markets. Any increase in uncertainty shifts the liquidity preference function, and this shift can be quite marked and sudden.

Obviously, the reverse--a decrease in uncertainty--can occur. If risk-averters are dominant then it is likely that an increase in uncertainty can be a rapid phenomenon, whereas a decrease will require a slow accretion of confidence. There is no need for a loss in confidence to proceed at the same pace as a gain in confidence.

Rapid changes in desired portfolios may be confronted with short-period inelastic supplies of primary assets, (real capital and government liabilities). As a result, the relative prices of different assets change. An increase in uncertainty will see the price of inside assets--real capital and equities--fall relative to the price of outside assets--government debt--and money; a decrease in uncertainty will see the price of inside assets rise relative to that of outside assets.

24/ See J. Tobin, "Liquidity Preference as Behavior Toward Risk," pp. 65-68.

The nominal money supply in our fractional reserve banking
system can be almost infinitely elastic. Any events that increase uncertainty on the part of owners of real wealth will also increase uncertainty of commercial bankers. Unless prices of inside assets are pegged
by the central bank, a sharp increase in uncertainty will result in the
price of inside assets falling relative to both money and the price of
default-free, or protected assets.

In a decentralized private enterprise economy with private
commercial banks, we cannot expect the money supply to increase sufficiently to offset the effects of a sharp increase in uncertainty upon
inside asset prices. Conversely we cannot expect the money supply to
fall sufficiently to offset the effects of a sharp decrease in uncertainty.
We should expect the private, profit-maximizing, risk-averting commercial
banks to behave perversely, in that with a decrease in uncertainty they
are willing and eager to increase the money supply and with an increase
in uncertainty they act to contract the money supply. [25]

Portfolios must hold the existing stocks of private real assets,
Treasury debt, and money. Even during an investment boom the annual
increment to the stock of real capital is small relative to the total

---

[25] The stagnant state that follows a deep depression has been characterized by very low yields--high prices--on default-free assets. One
interpretation of the liquidity trap is that it reflects the inability
to achieve a meaningful difference between the yields on real assets
and on default-free assets by further lowering of the yield on default-
free assets. An equivalent but more enlightening view of the liquidity
trap is that circumstances occur in which it is not possible by increasing
the stock of money to raise the price of the units in the stock of
existing capital so as to induce investment. In these conditions expansionary fiscal policy, especially government spending, will increase the cash
flows that units in the stock of real capital generate. In otherwise
stagnant conditions this realized improvement in earnings will tend to
increase the relative price of inside capital, and thus help induce
investment.

stock. However, in time the stock of reproducible capital is infinitely
elastic at the price of newly produced capital goods. Thus there is a
ceiling to the price of a unit of the stock of real capital in the current
market. This ceiling price allows for an expected decline in the price
of the stock to the price of the flow of newly produced units.

The current return on real capital collected in firms reflects
the current functioning of the economy, whether prosperity or depression
rules. During an investment boom current returns are high. Because a
ceiling on the price of units in the stock of capital is imposed by the
cost of investment, a shift in the desired composition of portfolios
towards a greater proportion of real capital cannot lower very far the
short-run yield on real capital valued at market price; in fact because
of prosperity and greater capacity utilization this yield may increase.
As the outside assets--Treasury debt and so forth--are now less desirable
than in other more uncertain circumstances, their yield must rise toward
equality with the yield on inside or real assets. To paraphrase Keynes
". . . in a world without uncertainty no one outside of a lunatic asylum. . ."
will hold Treasury bills as a store of wealth unless their yield is the
same as that on real assets.

As the implicit yield on money is primarily the value of the
implied insurance policy it embodies, a decrease in uncertainty lowers
this implicit yield and thus lowers the amount desired in portfolios. As
all money must be held, as bankers are eager to increase its supply, and
as its nominal value cannot decline, the money price of other assets, in
particular real assets, must increase.

In an euphoric economy it is widely thought that past doubts about the future of the economy were based upon error. The behavior of money and capital market interest rates during such a period is consistent with a rapid convergence of the yield upon default-free and default-possible assets. This convergence takes place by a decline in the price of--the rise in the interest rate on--default-free assets relative to the price of--yield on--the economy's underlying real capital.

In addition to default-free--government debt plus gold--and default-possible--real capital, private debts, equities--assets, there are protected assets. Protected assets in varying degrees and from various sources carry some protection against consequences that would follow from unfavorable events. Typical example of such assets are bonds and savings deposits.

Financial intermediaries--including banks as they emit money--generate assets that are at least partially protected. A rise in intermediation and particularly a rise in bank money, even if the asset acquired by the bank carries default possibilities, may 'unbalance' portfolios in favor of default-free assets. The ability of banking, through the creation of money, to stimulate an economy rests upon the belief that banks and the monetary authorities are able to give such protection to their liabilities. The liabilities of other financial intermediaries are protected, but not so much as bank money; thus their stimulative effect, while not negligible, is smaller. In an euphoric economy the value of such protection decreases, and these instruments also fall in price relative to real assets or equities.[26]

To summarize the relative prices of assets are affected by portfolio imbalance that follows from changing views as to uncertainty concerning future states of the economy. A decrease in the felt uncertainty will raise the price of units in the stock of real inside assets for any given supply of money, other outside assets, and assets that are in all or in part protected against the adverse behavior of the economy; an increase in felt uncertainty will lower these prices. For a given state of uncertainty and stock of real capital assets, the greater the quantity of money, other outside assets, and protected assets, the greater the price of units in the stock of real capital. Investment consists of producing substitutes for items in the stock of real capital; the price of the units in the stock is the demand price for units to be produced. To the extent that the supply of investment responds positively to its demand price, the pace of investment flows from portfolio imbalance.

The investment process can be detailed as (1) the portfolio balance relation that states the market price for capital assets as a function of the money supply (Diagram I) and (2) the investment supply

---

26/ Incidentally, the phenomenon by which a decrease in the value of some protection affects observable market prices also exists in the labor market. Civil servants and teachers accept low money incomes relative to others with the same initial job opportunity spectrum in exchange for security; civil servants value security more than others. In an euphoric, full employment economy the value of such civil servant security diminishes. Hence in order to attract workers, their relative measured market wage will need to rise.

function that states how much investment output will be produced at each
market price for capital assets (Diagram II). It is assumed that the
market price for capital assets is the demand price for investment output. The supply curve of investment output is positively sloped. At
some positive price the output of investment goods becomes zero. The
market price of capital assets as determined by portfolio preferences
is sensitive to the state of expectations or the degree of uncertainty
with respect to the future.[27/]

In Diagram I, I have chosen to keep the stock of capital constant.
Thus $V = P_k \bar{K} + M$, where V is wealth, P_k is price level of capital, $\bar{K}$ is
the fixed stock of capital, and M is outside money. As M increases, V
increases because of both the rise in M and a rise in P_k. If M increases
as manna from heaven, it would be appropriate for the consumption function
to include a W/P_y variable (P_y is the price level of current output).
This would, by today's conventions, add an upward drifting consumption
function to the mechanism by which a rise in M affects output.[28/]

27/ The 'investment' argument builds upon R.W. Clower, "An Investigation into
the Dynamics of Investment," and J. G. Witte, Jr., "The Microfoundations of
the Social Investment Function." Both Clower and Witte emphasize the determination of the price per unit of the stock as a function of exogenously
given interest rates: they are wedded to a productivity basis for the demand
for real capital assets. The argument here emphasizes the portfolio balance
or speculative aspects of the demand for real capital assets. Thus interest
rates are computed from the relation between expected flows and market prices,
that is, the price of capital as a function of the money supply relation is
the liquidity preference function.

28/ Alternatively the value of wealth can be kept constant; thus $\bar{V} = P_k K + M$.
An increase in M is initially an "open market operation" $\Delta M = P_k K$. However,
as 'portfolios' now hold more money and less capital goods, the price per unit
of capital goods rises. Capital is expropriated so that W remains fixed. This
is a pure portfolio balance relation.
    If, starting from an initial position, $V_o = P_{ko} K_o + M_o$, M is increased, the
the P_k of the second variant would lie above that of the first variant. If M
is decreased, the P_k of the second variant will lie below that of the first.
The constant wealth variant cuts the constant private capital stock variant
from below. I have assumed constant capital stock K in drawing Diagram I.

If C = f(Y) and Y = C + I, then the above determines income as a function of M.[29]

It is impossible in this view to generate an investment function I = f(r) that is independent of the portfolio adjustments of the liquidity preference doctrine; investment is a speculative activity in a capitalist economy that is only peripherally related to productivity.

Two phenomena can be distinguished. If M remains fixed as capital is accumulated, a slow downward drift of the Q (M,K) function (Diagram I) will take place. A rise in M is needed to maintain real asset prices in the face of the rise in the stock of real capital.[30] Alternatively, if portfolio preferences change, perhaps because of a change in uncertainty, then, independently of the impact of real accumulation, the $Q(M,\bar{K})$ function will shift. It is the second type of shift that occupies center stage in the Keynesian view of the world. And this has been neglected in both monetary and investment analysis.

---

[29] If we assume that the future expected returns from capital to be known, then the equation $P_k = Q (M,\bar{K})$ can be transformed into $r = Q (M,\bar{K})$. With every quantity of M a different price will be paid for the same future income stream; a larger quantity of money will be associated with a higher market price of existing capital and thus a lower rate of return on the market value of capital. In a similar way, the investment relation can be turned into an I = I (r) relationship. This requires the same information on expected returns as is used in transforming the portfolio relation. In turn the I = I (r) and the r = Q (M) can be transformed into I = Q (M). Because $\bar{K}$ and not Y is an argument in equation 1, the I-S, L-M construction is not obtained.

[30] Underlying preferences need not be such that for P_k to remain constant $\frac{dM}{M} = \frac{dK}{K}$; it may be that $\frac{dM}{M} < \frac{dK}{K}$ or even $\frac{dM}{M} > \frac{dK}{K}$ (see Arrow, "Aspects of the Theory of Risk Bearing"). Friedman's well-known result is that $\frac{dM}{M} > \frac{dP_kK}{P_kK}$.

See M. Friedman, "The Demand for Money: Some Theoretical and Empirical Results," pp. 327-51.

DIAGRAM I

Stock

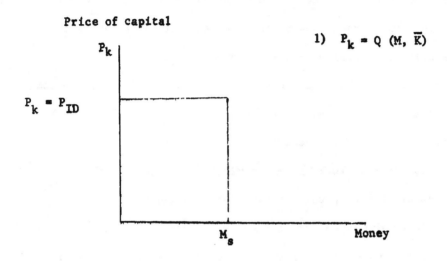

Price of capital

1) $P_k = Q (M, \bar{K})$

DIAGRAM II

Flow

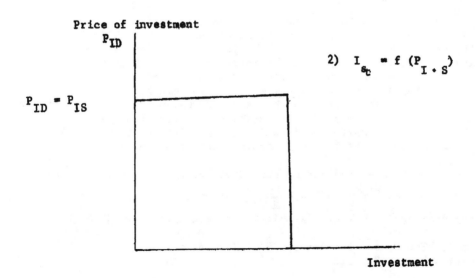

Price of investment

2) $I_{s_c} = f (P_{I \cdot S})$

At all times investment demand has to take into account the returns received during various expected states of the economy. As the result of a shock, the weight attached to depression returns may increase. As the dust settles there is gradual easing of the views on the likelihood of unfavorable states of nature. The weight attached to liquidity is decreased and a gradual increase of investment will take place.

Hopefully we know enough to supplement investment by honorary investments (Government spending) so that the expected returns from capital will not again reflect large-scale excess capacity. Nevertheless, if a shock takes place, some time elapses before its effects wear off. In these circumstances honorary investment may have to carry the burden of maintaining full employment for an extended period.

The essence of the argument is that investment activity may be viewed as an offshoot of portfolio preferences, and that portfolio preferences reflect the attempt by rational men to do well in a world with uncertainty. Any shock to portfolio preferences that leads to a sharp drop in investment results from experiences with portfolios that had gone sour. On a large scale, portfolios go sour in the aftermath of a financial crisis.

Appendix to Section IV: A Model

The model can be written as follows:

(1) $Y = C + I$

(2) $C = C(Y)$

(3) $I = I(P_{IS}, \overline{W})$

(4) $P_K = L(M, \overline{K})$

(5) $P_{I \cdot D} = P_K$

$$(6) \quad P_{IS} = P_{I \cdot D}$$

$$(7) \quad M_o = M_s$$

M_s (money), $\overline{K}$ (capital stock), and $\overline{W}$ (wages) are all exogenous, $P_M = 1$.

Symbols have their usual meaning: we add $P_{I \cdot S}$ as the supply price of a unit of investment, P_K as the market price of a unit of existing real or inside capital, and $P_{I \cdot D}$ is the demand price of a unit of investment.

$$(3) \quad \frac{dI}{dP_{IS}} > 0, \quad \left. \frac{P_{IS}}{I \to 0} \right. > 0, \quad \frac{dP_{IS}}{dW} > 0$$

$$(4) \quad \frac{dP_K}{dM} > 0, \quad \frac{dP_K}{dK} < 0$$

Equation 4 is unstable with respect to views as to uncertainty; it shifts "down" whenever uncertainty increases. This portfolio balance equation (the liquidity preference function) yields a market price for the units in the stock of real capital for each quantity of money.

Given W, I adjusts so that $P_{IS} = P_K$ (equations 3, 5, and 6). Once I is given C and Y are determined (equations 1 and 2). Nowhere in the above model does either the interest rate or the productivity of capital appear. "Liquidity preference" (equation 4) determines the market price of the stock of real assets. A shift in liquidity preference means a shift in equation 4, not a movement along the function.

In the above model, the tune is called by the market price of the stock of real capital. Given a cost curve for investment which has a positive price for zero output, it is possible for the demand price to fall below the price at which there will be an appreciable production of capital goods. Thus the 'complete' collapse of investment is possible.

Of course, productivity in the sense of the expected quasi-rents
is almost always an element in the determination of the market price of
a real asset or a collection of assets. However, this formulation minimizes
the impact of productivity as it emphasizes that the liquidity attribute
of assets may at times be of greater significance in determiming their
market price than their productivity. The perspective in this formulation
is that of business cycles, not of a full employment steady state.

Productivity of capital takes the form of expected future earnings
(gross profits after taxes) of a collection of capital goods within a producing unit. In any real world decision, the earnings on specific items
or collections of capital must be estimated, and the heterogeneity of the
capital stock must be taken into account.

Once earnings are estimated, then given the current market price,
a discount rate can be computed. That is, we have

$$(7) \quad P_k \cdot \bar{K} = \sum_{i=1}^{n} \sum_{t=1}^{t} Q_i/(1 + r_i)^t$$

which states the arithmetic relation that the value of the capital stock is
of necessity equal to the discounted value of some known stream of
returns, Q_i. If the current market determines $P_k \cdot K$ and if a set of
Q_i are estimated, an interest rate can be computed. If it is wished,
equation 4 can be suppressed by using equation 7 that is

$$(4') \quad \frac{1}{K} \sum_{i,t=1}^{n} \frac{Q_i}{(1+r_i)t} = L(M, K)$$

If a transaction demand for money is added, if the Q_i are interpreted as a function of Y, if all r_i are assumed equal, and if $\overline{K}$ is suppressed as being fixed in the short run then

(4") $M_0 = L(r, Y)$

may be derived.

For the investment decision, we may assume that the future return of the increment to capital is the same as to the stock of capital. With the Q_i known and assumed independent of the short-run pace of investment, then

(3') $P_{IS} = \dfrac{1}{\overline{K}} \displaystyle\sum_{i,\,t=1}^{n} \dfrac{Q}{(1+r_i)^t}$

Thus given the fact that the supply price of investment rises with investment (constant W), greater investment is associated with a lower interest rate. That is,

(3") $I = I(r,Y)$ and $\dfrac{dI}{dr} < o$

Both 4" and 3" are arithmetic transformations of 4 and 3. Equations 4 and 3 represent market phenomena, whereas 4" and 3' are computed transformations of market conditions.

For financial contracts such as bonds the Q_i are stated in the contract. Even so the yield to maturity is a computed number - the market number is the price of the bond.

When the interest rate is not computed, the investment decision and its relation to liquidity preference are viewed in a more natural way. Of course, for real capital the Q_i reflects the productivity in the form of cash flows, current and expected. But the productivity of capital and investment affect present performance only after they are filtered through an evaluation of the state of the irrational, uncertain world that is the positioning variable in the liquidity preference function. Productivity and thrift exist, but in a capitalist economy their impact is always filtered by uncertainty.

V.   How Does Tight Money Work?

Tight money, defined as rising nominal interest rates associated
with stricter other terms on contracts, may work to restrain demand in two
ways. [31/]   In the conventional view tight money operates through rationing
demand by means of rising interest rates.   Typically this has been represented by movements along a stable negatively sloped demand curve for
investment (and some forms of consumption) that is drawn as a function of
the interest rate.   An alternative view that follows from the argument in
Section IV, envisages tight money as inducing a change in "expectations,"
in the perceived uncertainty, due to an episode such as a financial crisis
or a period of financial stringency.   This can within Diagrams 1 and 2 of
Section IV be represented by a downward shift in the infinitely elastic
demand curve for investment.

The way in which tight money operates depends upon the state of
the economy.   In a non-euphoric expanding economy, where liability structures
are considered satisfactory, monetary restraint will likely operate by way
of rationing along a stable investment demand curve.   In a booming euphoric
economy, where high and rising prices of capital are associated with a
willingness on the part of firms to "extend" their liability structures
and of financial intermediaries to experiment with both their assets and
their liabilities, tight money will be effective only if it brings such

---

31/   "Tightness" of money refers to costs (including contract terms) for
financing activity by way of debt.   High and rising interest rates plus
more restrictive other terms on contracts are evidence of tight money.
Tightness has nothing directly to do with the rate of change of the money
supply or the money base or what you will.   Only as these money supply
phenomena affect contract terms do they affect tightness.

Nonprice rationing by suppliers of finance means that the other terms
in financing contracts for some demanders increase markedly.   The tightness
of money is not measured correctly when only one term in a contract, the
interest rate, is considered.

portfolio, or financial structure, experimentation to a halt. A reconsideration of the desirability of financial experimentation will not take
place without a triggering event and the reaction can be both quick and
disastrous. A euphoric boom is characterized by a stretching, or thinning
out, of liquidity; the end of a boom occurs when desired liquidity quickly
becomes significantly greater than actual liquidity.

In a euphoric economy, with ever increasing confidence, there is
an increase in the weights attached to the occurrence of states of nature
favorable to the owning of larger stocks of real capital. In these circumstances, an upward drift in the price of real capital-money supply
function (Diagram I, p. 34) will take place.

This shift means that for all units both the expected flows of
cash from operations and the confidence in these expectations are rising.
Given these expectations, an enterprise assumes that with safety it can
undertake (1) to emit liabilities whose cash needs will be met by these now-
confidently-expected cash flows and (2) to undertake projects with the
expectation that the cash flows from operations will be one of the sources
of finance. In a euphoric economy the weight attached to the necessity
for cash reserves to ease strains due to unexpected shortfalls in cash
flows is ever decreasing.

In a lagless world - where all investment decisions are taken,
so to speak, with a clean slate - current investment spending is related
to current expectations and financial or money market conditions. In a
world when today's investment spending reflects past decisions, the
needs for financing today can often be quite inelastic with respect to

today's financing conditions: and today's financing conditions, may have their major effect upon investment spending in the future. Thus there exists a pattern of lags between money and capital market conditions and investment spending conditions. This lag pattern is not independent of economic events. A dramatic financial market event, in particular a financial crisis or widespread distress, can have a quick effect.

For units with outstanding debts, tight money means that cash payment commitments rise as positions are refinanced. This is true not only because interest rates are higher but also because other terms of the units' borrowing contracts are affected. In addition if projects are undertaken with the expectation that they would be financed in part by cash generated by ongoing operations, and if the available cash flows fall short of expectations--due perhaps to the increased cost of the refinanced inherited debt--then a larger amount will need to be financed by debt or by the sale of financial assets. This means that the resultant balance sheet can be inferior to and the cash flow commitments larger than the target envisaged when the project was undertaken. Conversely if gross profits rise faster than costs, so that a smaller-than-expected portion of investment is financed by debt, the resultant balance sheet will be superior to that expected when projections were made. In this way, investment may be retarded or accelerated by cash flow and balance sheet considerations.[32]

---

[32] For a more detailed analysis of how financial actualities may relate to project decisions, see H. P. Minsky, "Financial Intermediation in the Money and Capital Markets." See also E. Greenberg, "A Stock-Adjustment Investment Model."

Deposit financial institutions are especially vulnerable to tight money if their assets are of significantly longer term than their debts; they are virtually refinancing their position daily by offering terms that aee attractive to their depositors. A rapid rise in their required cash flows due to interest costs may take place, which can lead to a sharp reduction in their net income.

Thus during a euphoric expansion the effects of tight money are more than offset for units holding real capital, whereas for other units, such as savings banks, tight money means a significant deterioration in their financial position whether measured by liquidity or net worth.

In a euphoric economy the willingness to hold money or near money decreases. The observed tightness of money - the rise in interest rates on near monies and other debts - is not necessarily caused by any undue constraint upon the rate of increase of the money supply; rather it reflects the rapid increase in the demand for financing. An attempt by the authorities to sate the demand for finance by creating bank credit will lead to rapidly rising prices: inflationary expectations will add to the euphoria. Euphoric expectations will not be ended by a fall in income, as the strong investment demand that is calling the tune is insensitive to the rise in financing terms.

In a euphoric economy, characterized by an investment boom, cash payments become ever more closely articulated to cash receipts: the speculative stock of money and near monies is depleted. Two phenomena follow from this closer articulation. The size of both the shortfall

in cash receipts and of the overrun in cash payments due to normal
operations that will result in insufficient cash on hand to meet payments decreases. The frequency with which refinancing or asset sales
are necessary to meet payment commitments increases. Units become
more dependent upon the normal functioning of various financial markets.

Under these emerging circumstances there is a decrease in the
size of the dislocation that can cause serious financial difficulties
to a unit, and an increase in the likelihood that a unit in difficulty
will set other units in difficulty. Also even local or sectoral financial distress or market disruptions may induce widespread attempts to gain
liquidity by running off or selling out positions in real or financial
assets (inventory liquidation). This action in turn may depress incomes
and market prices of real and financial assets. We may expect financial
institutions to react to such developments by trying to clean up their
balance sheets and to reverse the portfolio changes entered into during
the recent euphoric period. The simultaneous attempt by financial institutions, consumers, and firms to improve their balance sheets may lead to a
rupture of what had been normal as well as standby financing relations.
As a result losses occur, and these, combined with the market disruptions,
induce a more conservative view as to the desired liability structure.

The view that, in conditions of euphoria, tight money operates
by causing a re-evaluation of the uncertainties carried by economic
units is in marked contrast to the textbook analysis of tight money
seen as operating by constraining expenditures along a stable investment

function. If an expansion is taking place in the absence of a transformation, by way of euphoric expectations, of preferred portfolios and liability structures then the system can operate by rationing along a stable investment relation. Then tight money may lead to a decline in investment and a relaxation of monetary constraint may reverse this decline: conventional monetary policy can serve as an economic steering wheel.

But once the expansion is associated with the transformation of asset and liability structures that have been identified as characteristic of an euphoric economy, tight money will constrain demand only if it induces a shift either in the demand function for money or in the price function for capital goods. For this to happen the expansion must continue long enough for balance sheets to be substantially changed. Then some triggering event that induces a reconsideration of desired balance sheets must occur. A financial crisis or at least some significant amount of financial distress is needed to dampen the euphoria. The fear of financial failure must be credible in order to overcome expectations built on a long record of success.

During an emerging euphoric boom, the improvement in expectations may overwhelm rising interest rates. As a result of the revision of portfolio standards, the supply of finance seems to be almost infinitely elastic at stepwise rising rates. Typically this "infinitely" elastic supply is associated with the emergence of new financial instruments and institutions, such as the use of Federal funds to make position, the explosive growth of negotiable CD's, and the development of a second banking system.[33]

---

[33] H. P. Minsky, "Central Banking and Money Market Changes."

Under these circumstances a central bank will see its restriction
of the rate of growth of the money supply or the reserve base overwhelmed
by the willingness of consumers, business firms, and financial institutions
to decrease cash balances: increases in velocity overcome restrictions in
quantity. The frustrated central bank can try to compensate for its lack
of success in constraining expansion by further decreasing the rate of
growth of the money supply, thus forcing a more rapid development of a
very tightly articulated cash positions. Such a further tightening will
occur within a financial environment that is increasingly vulnerable to
disruption. Under these circumstances the transition will not be from too
rapid economic expansion to stability by way of a slow deceleration, but
a rapid decline will follow a sharp braking of the expansion.

With some form of a financial crisis likely to occur after an
euphoric boom, it becomes difficult to prescribe the correct policy for
a central bank. However, the central bank must be aware of this
possibility and it must stand ready to act as a lender of last resort to
the financial system as a whole if and when a break takes place. With
the path of the economy independent in its gross terms of the rate of
increase of the money supply and of the relative importance of bank
financing, the central bank might as well resist the temptation to further
tighten its constraints if the initial extent of constraint does not work
quickly. The central bank should sustain the rate of growth of the reserve
base and the money supply at a rate consistent with the long-term growth
of the economy. This course should be adopted in the hope, however slight,

that the rise in velocity - deterioration of balance sheets phenomena described above--will converge, by a slow deceleration of the euphoric expectations, to a sustainable steady state.

In particular during a euphoric expansion the central bank should resist the temptation to introduce constraining direct controls on that part of the financial system most completely under its control--the commercial banks. The central bank should recognize that a euphoric expansion will be a period of innovation and experimentation by both bank and nonbank financial institutions. From the perspective of picking up the pieces, restoring confidence, and sustaining the economy, the portion of the financial system that the central bank most clearly protects should be as large as possible. Instead of constraining commercial banks by direct controls, the central bank should aim at sustaining the relative importance of commercial banks even during a period of euphoric expansion; in particular the commercial banks should not be unduly constrained from engaging in rate competition for resources.

VI.   The Theory of Financial Instability

In section IV it was concluded that normal functioning requires
that the price level, perhaps implicit, of the stock of real capital
assets be consistent with the supply price of investment goods at the
going-wage level. The euphoric boom occurs when portfolio preferences
change so that the price level of the stock rises relative to the wage level,
causing an increase in the output of investment goods. A sharp fall in the
price level of the stock of real assets will lead to a marked decline in
investment and thus in income: a deep depression can occur only if such
a change in relative prices takes place.

A.   Introduction

In the discussion of uncertainty, we identified one élement that
could lead to a sharp lowering of the price level of the existing stock of
capital. A sharp change in the desired composition of assets in portfolios--
due to an evaporation of confidence in views held previously as to the
likelihood of various alternative possible state-dates of the economy--
will lower the value of real assets relative to both the price level of
current output and money. Such a revaluation of the confidence with which
a set of expectation are held does not just happen.

The event that marks the change in portfolio preferences is a
period of financial crisis, distress, or stringency (used as descriptive
terms for different degrees of financial difficulty). However, a financial
crisis--used as a generic term--is not an accidental event, and not all
financial structures are equally prone to financial instability. Our
interest now is in these attributes of the financial system that determine
its stability.

We are discussing a system that is not globally stable. The economy is best analyzed by assuming that there exists more than one stable equilibrium for the system. We are interested in the determinants of the domain of stability around the various stable equilibria. Our questions are of the form: "What is the maximum displacement that can take place and still have the system return to a particular initial equilibrium point?" and "Upon what does this 'maximum displacement' depend?"

The maximum shock that the financial system may absorb and still have the economy return to its initial equilibrium depends upon the financial structure and the linkages between the financial structure and real income. Two types of shocks that can trigger large depressive movements of financial variables can be identified: one is a shortfall of cash flows due to an over-all drop in income, and the second is the distress of a unit due to "error" of management. But not all recessions trigger financial instability and not every financial failure, even of large financial units, triggers a financial panic or crisis. For not unusual events to trigger the unusual, the financial environment within which the potential triggering event occurs must have a sufficiently small domain of stability.

The contention in this paper is that the domain of stability of the financial system is mainly an endogenous phenomenon that depends upon liability structures and institutional arrangements. The exogenous elements in determining the domain of financial stability are the government and central banking arrangements: after mid-1966 it is clear that the exogenous policy instrument of deposit insurance is a powerful offset to events with the potential for setting off a financial crisis.

There are two basic attributes of the financial system that
determine the domain of stability of the financial system: (1) the extent
to which a close articulation exists between the contractual and customary
cash flows from a unit and its various cash receipts and (2) the weight
in portfolios of those assets that in almost all circumstances can be sold
or pledged at well nigh their book or face value. A third element, not
quite so basic, that determines vulnerability to a financial crisis is the
extent to which expectations of growth and of rising asset prices have
affected current asset prices and the values at which such assets enter the
financial systems.[34/] The domain of stability of the financial system is
smaller the closer the articulation of payments, the smaller the weight
of protected assets, and the larger the extent to which asset prices reflect
both growth expectations and realized past appreciations. The evolution of
the above attributes of the financial structure over time will affect the
size of the domain of stability of the financial system. An hypothesis
of this, as well as the earlier presentations of these ideas is that when
full employment is being sustained by private demand, the domain of
stability of the financial system decreases.

In addition to the impact of such full employment a euphoric
economy with its demand-pull tight money will be accompanied by a rapid

---

34/ Assets enter the financial system when they are used as collateral
for borrowing. A newly built house enters the financial system through
its mortgage, which is based upon its current production costs. If the
expectation takes over that house prices will rise henceforth at say 10
per cent a year, the market value of existing houses will rise to reflect
the expected capital gains. If mortgages are based upon purchase prices,
once such a house turns over, the values in the portfolios of financial
institutions reflect growth expectations. This happens with takeovers,
mergers, conglomerates, and so on. It is no accident that such corporate
developments are most frequent during euphoric periods.

increase in the layering of financial obligations, which also tends to
decrease the domain of stability. For as layering increases the close-
ness with which payments are articulated to receipts increases and
layering increases the ratio of inside assets to those assets whose nominal
or book value will not be affected by system behavior.[35/] A euphoric
economy will typically be associated with a stock market boom and an
increase in the proportion of the value of financial assets that is sensitive to a sharp revaluation of expectations.

Even though a prolonged expansion, dominated by private demand,
will bring about a transformation of portfolios and changes in asset
structures conducive to financial crises, the transformations in portfolios
that take place under euphoric conditions sharply accentuate such trends.
It may be conjectured that euphoria is a necessary prelude to a financial
crisis and that euphoria is almost an inevitable consequence of the
successful functioning of an enterprise economy.

Thus the theory of financial stability takes into account two
aspects of the behavior of a capitalist economy. The first is the
evolution of the financial structure over a prolonged expansion, which
affects the nature of the primary assets, the extent of financial layering
and the evolution of financial institutions and usages. The second consists
of the financial impacts over a short period due to the existence of a highly
optimistic, euphoric economy; the euphoric economy is a natural consequence
of the economy doing well over a prolonged period. Over both the prolonged

---

35/ The relevant assets structure concept is outside assets as a ratio to
the combined assets (or liabilities) of all private units, not the consolidated assets.

boom and the euphoric period portfolio transformations occur that
decrease the domain of stability of the financial system.

Financial instability as a system characteristic is compounded
of two elements. How are units placed in financial distress and how does
unit distress escalate into a systemwide crisis?

B. The "banking theory" for all units

It is desirable to analyze all economic units as if they were a
bank - or at least a financial intermediary. The essential characteristic
of such a financial unit is that it finances a position by emitting
liabilities. A financial institution does not expect to meet the commitments stated in its liabilities by selling out its position, or allowing
its portfolio to run off. Rather it expects to refinance its position by
emitting new debt. On the other hand every unit, including banks and other
financial units, has a normal functioning cash flow from operations. The
relation between the normal functioning cash flow to and the refinancing
opportunities on the one hand and the commitments embodied in the liabilities
on the other determine the conditions under which the organization can
be placed in financial distress.

It is important for our purpose to look at all organizations from
the defensive viewpoint: "What would it take to put the organization in
financial distress?" This aspect will be made clearer when we discuss bank
and other examination procedures.

1. Solvency and Liquidity Constraints.

All economic units have a balance sheet. Given the valuation of
assets and liabilities one may derive a net worth or owner's equity for the

unit. The conditional maximization of owner's equity may be the proximate goal of business management - the condition reflecting the need to protect some minimum owner's equity under the most adverse contingency as to the state of the economy.

A unit is solvent, given a set of valuation procedures, when its net worth is positive.[36] A unit is liquid when it can meet its payment commitments. Solvency and liquidity are two conditions that all private economic organizations must always satisfy. Failure to satisfy either condition, or even coming close to failing, can lead to actions by others that affect profoundly the status of the organization.

Even though textbooks may consider solvency and liquidity as independent attributes, the two are interrelated. First of all, the willingness to hold the debt of any organization depends in part upon the protection to the debt holder embodied in the unit's net worth. A decline in net worth - perhaps the result of revaluation of assets - can lead to a decreased willingness to hold debts of a unit and hence to difficulties when it needs to refinance a position. A lack of liquidity may result from what was initially a solvency problem.

Similarly a net drain or outflow of cash from an organization may lead to a need to do the unusual - to acquire cash by selling assets. If, because of the thinness of the market, a sharp fall in the asset price occurs when such sales are essayed then a sharp drop in net worth takes place, especially if the organization is highly levered.

We can identify therefore, three sources of a decline in the price level of the stock (capital), relative, of course, to the flow (income and

36/ The common valuation procedures take book or market value. For purposes of both management and central bank decisions it would be better if valuation procedures were conditional, that is, of the form: if the economy behaves as follows, then these assets would be worth as follows.

investment). One is a rise in the weight attached to those possible states
of the society which make it disadvantageous to hold real assets, and financial assets whose value is closely tied to that of real assets. The second
is the fall in asset values due to a rise in the discount caused by uncertainty. The third is a decline in asset values as the conditions change
under which a position in these assets may be financed. In particular,
whenever the need to meet the cash payment commitments stated by liabilities
requires the selling out of a position, there is the possibility of a sharp
fall in the price of the positioned asset. Such a fall in asset prices
trigger a serious impact of financial markets upon demand for current output.

　　　2. The Need for Cash for Payments.

　　　Cash is needed for payments, which are related to financial as well
as income transactions. The layering of financial interrelations affects
the total payments that must be made. To the extent that layering increases
at a faster rate than income, over a prolonged boom, or in response to
rising interest rates or during a euphoric period the payments/income ratio
will rise. The closer the articulation by consumers and business firms of
income receipts with payments due to financial contracts, the greater the
potential for financial crisis.

　　　Each money payment is a money receipt. As layering increases, the
importance of the uninterrupted flow of receipts increases· The inability
of one unit to meet its payment commitments affects the ability of the
would-be recipient unit to meet its payment commitments.

Three payment types can be distinguished: income, balance sheet, and portfolio, each of which can in turn be broken down into subclasses.[37] These payment types reflect the fact that economic units have incomes and manage portfolios.

The liabilities in a portfolio state the payment commitments. These contractual payment commitments can be separated into dated, demand, and contingent commitments. To each liability some penalty is attached for not meeting the commitment: and the payment commitments quite naturally fall into classes according to the seriousness of the default penalty. In particular the payment commitments that involve the pledging of collateral are important - for they provide a direct and quick link between a decline in market value of assets and the need to make cash payments. That is, they are a type of contingent payment commitment that involves the supply of additional collateral or cash whenever a market price falls below some threshhold. This margin or collateral maintenance payment commitment can be a source of considerable disorganization and can lead to sharp declines in asset prices.

37/ Income payments are those payments directly related to the production of current income. Even though some labor costs are independent of current output, the data are such that all wage payments are in the income payments class. All of the 'Leontief' payments for purchased inputs are such income payments.

Balance sheet payments during a period are those payments that reflect past financial commitments. Lease, interest, and repayment of principal are among balance sheet payments. For a financial intermediary either withdrawals by depositors or loans to policyholders are balance sheet payments.

Portfolio payments are due to transactions in real and financial assets.

Any payment may be of a different class when viewed by the payor or the payee. To the producer of investment goods the receipts from the sale of the good is an income receipt, to the purchaser it is a portfolio payment.

In addition to types, payments may be classified by "from whom" and "to whom."

If money consisted solely of deposits subject to check, then total payments would be the total debits to accounts and total receipts would be credits to accounts. Hence, it is the implication for system stability of total clearings, where the financial footings are integrated with the income footings, that is being examined.

Another aspect of balance sheet payment commitments is the source

of the cash that will be used to make the payments. Three sources can be

distinguished: the flow due to the generation of income; the flow due to

the assets held in a portfolio; and the flow due to transactions in assets,

either the emission of new liabilities or the sale of assets.

For each unit, or class of units, the trend in payment commitments

relative to actual or potential sources of cash generates the changing

structure of financial interrelations. The basic empirical hypothesis is

that over a prolonged expansion - and in particular during a euphoric period -

the balance sheet commitments to make payments increases faster than income

receipts for private units (layering increases faster than income) and so

total financial commitments rise relative to income. In addition, during

euphoric periods, portfolio payments (transactions in assets) increase relative

to both income and financial transactions. The measured rise in income

velocity during an expansion underestimates the increase in the payment load

being carried by the money supply. [38]

C. Modes of system behavior

Three modes of system behavior can be distinguished depending upon

how ex-post savings are in fact offset by ex-post investment. The offsets

to saving that we will consider are investment in real private capital and

Government deficits. For convenience we will call real private capital

---

[38] In various places, I have tried to estimate by proxies some of these
relations. Empirical investigation of stability could begin with a more
thorough and also an up-to-date examination of these payment relations.
The relations mentioned in this section are discussed in detail in my paper,
"Financial Crisis, Financial Systems, and the Performance of the Economy "
op. cit.

inside assets and the accumulated total of Government deficits outside assets. Thus the consolidated change in net worth in an economy over a time period equals the change in the value of inside assets plus the change in the value of outside assets.

At any moment in time the total private net worth of the system equals the consolidated value of outside plus inside assets. Assuming the value of outside assets is almost independent of system behavior, the ratio of the value of outside to the value of total or inside assets in the consolidated accounts is one gross measure of the financial structure.

The savings of any period are offset by outside and inside assets. The ratio of outside to inside assets in the current offset to savings as compared to the initial ratio of outside to inside assets will determine the "financial bias" of current income. If the Government deficit is a larger portion of the current offset to savings than it is of the initial wealth structure, then the period is biased toward outside assets; if it is smaller, the period is biased towards inside assets; and if it is the same, then the period is neutral.

Over a protracted expansion the bias in financial development is toward inside assets. This bias is compounded out of three elements:

(1) Current savings are allocated to private investment rather than to Government deficits.

(2) Capital gains raise the market price of the stock of inside assets.

(3) Increases in interest rates lower the nominal value of outside, income-earnings assets. Thus the vulnerability of portfolios to declines

in the market price of the constituent assets increases.[39]

In the long run portfolio balance has been maintained by cycles in the relative weights of primary assets accumulated: historically the portfolio cycle centered around business cycles of deep depressions. However, to judge what is happening over time it is necessary to evaluate the significance of changes in financial usages. The existence of effective deposit insurance makes the inside assets owned by the banking system at least a bit outside. The same is true for all other Government underwritings and endorsements of private debt. Thus with the growth of Government and Government agency contingent liabilities even growth that is apparently biased toward the emission of private liabilities may in fact be biased toward outside assets. An attempt to enumerate - and then evaluate - the various Government endorsements and underwritings of various asset and financial markets in these terms is necessary when estimating the potential of an economy for financial instability.

D. Secondary markets

The domain of stability of the system depends upon the ratio of the value of those assets whose market value is independent of system behavior to the value of those assets whose market value reflects expected system behavior. The value of a particular asset can be independent of system behavior either because its market is pegged or because the flow of

---

[39] This is, of course, an assertion as to the facts, and the truth of these statements can be tested. Perhaps with a government sector that is 10 per cent of GNP, such statements are less true than with one that is 1 per cent of GNP.

payments that will be made does not depend upon system performance and its capital value is largely independent of financial market conditions.

For secondary markets to be an effective determinant of system stability they must transform an asset into a reliable source of cash for a unit whenever needed. This means that the secondary market must be a dealer market; in other words, there needs to be a set of position takers who will buy significant amounts for their own account and who sell out of their own stock of assets. Such position takers must be financed. Presumably under normal functioning the position taker is financed by borrowing from banks, financial intermediaries, and other private cash sources. However, a venturesome, reliable position taker must have adequate standby or emergency financing sources. The earlier argument about refinancing a position applies with special force to any money market or financial market dealer.

The only source of refinancing that can be truly independent of any epidemics of confidence or lack of confidence in financial markets is the central bank. Thus if the set of protected assets is to be extended by the organization of secondary markets, the stability of the financial system will be best increased if the dealers in these secondary markets have guaranteed access to the central bank.

It might be highly desirable to have the normal functioning of the system encompass dealer intermediaries who finance a portion of their position directly at the Federal Reserve discount window.

If a Federal Reserve peg existed in the market for some class of private liabilities, these liabilities would become guaranteed sources of cash at guaranteed prices. Such assets are at least in part outside, and they would increase the domain of stability of the system for any structure of other liabilities.

The extension of secondary markets to new classes of assets and the associated opening of the discount window to new financial intermediaries may compensate at least in part - or may even more than compensate - for the changes in financial structure due to the dominance of private investment in the offsets to saving during a prolonged boom.

E.   Unit and system instability

Financial vulnerability exists when the tolerance of the financial system to shocks has been decreased due to three phenomena that cumulate over a prolonged boom: (1) the growth of financial--balance sheet and portfolio--payments relative to income payments; (2) the decrease in the relative weight of outside and guaranteed assets in the totality of financial asset values; and (3) the building into the financial structure of asset prices that reflect boom or euphoric expectations. The triggering device in financial instability may be the financial distress of a particular unit.

In such a case, the initiating unit, after the event, will be adjudged guilty of poor management. However, the poor management of this unit or even of many units, may not be the cause of system instability. System instability occurs when the financial structure is such that the impact of the initiating units upon other units will lead to other units being placed in difficulty or becoming tightly pressed.

One general systemwide contributing factor to the development of a crisis will be a decline in income. A high financial commitment-income ratio seems to be a necessary condition for financial instability; a decline in national income would raise this ratio and would tend to put units in difficulty. Attempts by units with shrunken income to meet their commitments by selling assets adversely affects other initially quite liquid or solvent organizations and has a destabilizing impact upon financial markets. Thus explosive process involving declining asset prices and income flows may be set in motion.

The liabilities of banks and nonbank financial intermediaries are considered by other units (1) as their reservoirs of cash for possible delays in income and financial receipts and (2) as an asset that will never depreciate in nominal value. Bank and financial intermediary failure has an impact upon many units - more units hold liabilities of these institutions than hold liabilities of other private sector organizations. In addition such failures by calling into question the soundness of the asset structure of all units, tend to modify all desired portfolios. A key element in the escalation of financial distress to systemwide instability and crisis is the appearance of financial distress among financial institutions. Without the widespread losses and changes in desired portfolios that follows a disruption of the financial system, it is difficult for a financial crisis to occur. The development of effective central banking, which makes less likely a pass through to other units of losses due to the failure of financial institutions should decrease the likelihood of the occurrence of sweeping financial instability that has characterized history.

From our analysis of uncertainty it appears that even if effective action by the central bank aborts a full-scale financial crisis by sustaining otherwise insolvent or illiquid organizations, the situation that made such

aborting activity necessary will cause private liability emitters, financial
intermediaries, and the ultimate holders of assets to now desire more conservative balance sheet structures. The movement toward more conservative
balance sheets will lead to a period of relative stagnation.

The following propositions seem to follow from the above analysis:

1. The domain of stability of the financial system is endogenous
and decreases during a prolonged boom.

2. A necessary condition for a deep depression is a prior financial
crisis.

3. The central bank does have the power to abort a financial crisis.

4. Even if a financial crisis is aborted by central bank action,
the tremor that goes through the system during the abortion can lead to a
recession that, while more severe than the mild recessions that occur with
financial stability, can be expected nevertheless to be milder and significantly
shorter than the great depressions of the past. [40]

---

[40] The above was written in the fall of 1966. If the crunch of 1966 is
identified as an aborted financial crisis, then the events of 1966-67 can
be interpreted as a particularly apt use of central bank and fiscal policy
to first abort a financial crisis and then offset the subsequent decline in
income. It is also evident from the experience since 1966 that if a crisis
and serious recession are aborted, the euphoria, now combined with inflationary expectations, may quickly take over again. It may be that for the
boom and inflationary expectations evident in 1969 to be broken the possibility
of a serious depression taking place again must become a credible threat.
Given the experience of the 1960's, it may also be true that the only way such
a threat may be made credible is to have a serious depression.

VII.   An Aside on Bank Examination.

Commercial banks and other deposit institutions are periodically examined.   I do not intend to offer a critique of current bank examination objectives and techniques or to inquire into whether it is useful or necessary.   I assume that bank examination will continue and that the only negotiable issue is its nature.

As now carried out, bank examinations enable the examining authority to determine the creditworthiness of the institution and to inform the public that mismanagement and fraud are not obvious.   The determination of credit-worthiness is an extension of the lender-borrower relationship, and the examination for fraud and mismanagement is a consumer protection function. It is argued here that a bank examination procedure that focuses on cash flow relationships can be a useful source of information for Federal Reserve policymaking.

Typically the end result of a bank examination is a balance sheet, which places prices on assets.   Many assets of financial institutions - such as bank loans - do not have an active market.   Such assets are priced at their face value, especially if they are current, even though they would sell, if a market existed, at a discount.[41/]   Items that are not current - what some call scheduled items - are valued at some arbitrary ratio to face value in arriving at the balance sheet.   An excess proportion of scheduled items is taken as indicating a need for corrective action by the institution. It is obvious that the examiners' balance sheet reflects many arbitrary rules,

---

41/   Of course, with a decline in market interest rates, the assets would sell at a premium.   The bias in writing this report has been to examine the effect of monetary constraint and rising interest rates.   This essay is a creature of its time—midyear to fall 1966.

especially to the extent that valuation is divorced from current market prices. An arbitrary element enters into every placing of a price on assets for which no broad, deep, and resilient market exists.

In addition measures of the adequacy of capital and liquidity are derived. These measures reflect examiner's experience. It may be that an examination procedure that focuses on cash flows will lead to a more precise evaluation of capital adequacy and liquidity.

Even though the value placed upon a financial asset may be the result of an arbitrary valuation procedure, the commitments of the emitter of the instrument are precise. The commitments are to make payments - either at specified dates, on demand, or upon the occurrence of some stated contingency. Both assets and liabilities of a financial institution are such contracts. The examiner, by reading the outstanding contracts, can make a time profile of contractually dated cash flows to and cash flows from the unit. Each profile of dated payments and receipts needs to be supplemented by behavioral relations detailing the conditions under which demand and contingent clauses of contracts will be exercised. Thus a time series of the needs and sources of cash, under alternative contingencies, can be estimated.[42]

Cash flow analysis enables the authorities to receive information about the expected impact of various economic policy operations upon the cash flow to and the cash flow from various units and classes of units. Whereas

[42] Computer technology makes such a transformation of the examination procedure from an analysis of values to an analysis of cash flows more feasible. The emphasis upon capital values in bank and similar examination procedure, as well as in economic analysis, may well reflect what were at one time insurmountable computational difficulties.

balance sheet analysis is essentially static, a cash flow analysis of any
financial organization that forecasts cash flows at some future date must
be based of necessity upon clearly stated assumptions as to (1) the values that certain
systemwide variables and (2) the functional relationships between these
variables and the elements of the unit's cash flows. The conditional nature
of any single statement makes it necessary to vary the assumptions - to
map out how changes in parameters of the assumed functions and in systemwide
variables affect cash flows. An evaluation of the expected cash status of
any institution, or class of institutions, will depend upon assumptions as
to how the different market-determined variables will behave. Thus the
examination procedure will have to embody the results of serious economic
analysis. Bank and other examination procedures should be forward looking.
That is, instead of asking questions about the present status and the past
history of an organization, the questions should be of the following form:
"Given the present status as an initial condition, what would be the dated
impacts upon the organization of various economic system, financial market,
and management developments?" The vulnerability of say the New York mutual
savings banks to rapidly rising interest rates on time deposits and the
sensitivity of the income and liquidity of West Coast savings institutions
to a decrease in the rate of growth of the local economy would have been
obvious with such an analysis.

     The proposed examination procedure becomes an analysis of the unit
that is conditional upon the behavior of the economy. Economic policy
decisions cannot be made on an adequate factual basis without some

knowledge of their impact upon various classes of financial institutions. Much of what happens seems to surprise the authorities: an adequate examination procedure would minimize such surprise.

Cash flow analysis transforms every asset into a generator of a cash flow to the organization. Financial assets may be subdivided into three classes depending on how they generate cash: cash itself, loans, and investments. There is no need to discuss cash itself. Loans are those assets that generate a contractual cash flow. The ability of the owning organization to accelerate this cash flow by sale is very restricted. We may as well assume that it does not exist. However, such assets may serve as collateral for loans, for example at the discount window. Investments, while they do embody contractual cash flows, may also be saleable in a market. Their current market price more or less states the cash flow that the managers can generate if they choose to sell out their position. True investments would have broad, deep, and resilient markets. Those of many banks and other financial institutions have thin markets, and the relevant cash flow to the organization from such investments follows from the contractual, rather than the marketable, properties of the asset.

Whereas current assets yield a cash flow to an organization, the process of asset acquisition results in a cash flow from the organization. As a continuing organization at each point in time a bank will have dated, demand, and contingent commitments to acquire assets. The commitments will be both explicit--lines of credit or letters--or implicit the result of a long-term financial relation between the bank and the potential

borrower.   Banks may similarly have an implicit commitment to bid for local
municipal issues.[43]/

The cash flow to an organization due to financial asset holdings
reflects both the flow of income and the repayment of principal. However
this division is not really relevant - what is relevant is the amount that
is available from any cash flow for the acquisition of new assets. That
is the cash flow to must be related to the cash flow from.

The debt liabilities of deposit and other financial intermediaries are commitments to pay cash - at some specified date, on demand,
or upon the occurrence of some contingency. These commitments include
both the repayment of principal and interest payments; although for many
deposit institutions interest payments are credited to the depositors'
account and do not generate an automatic cash drain.

The debt liabilities of deposit institutions can be separated
into service and purchased liabilities. Local demand deposits and passbook
savings are almost all service deposits. The volume of such deposits will
depend upon the state of the local economy and the action of local competitors.

43/ For all economic units, such continuing financial contacts and relations
are valuable assets. True, implicit agreements can be not honored if a
liquidity squeeze occurs but this imposes capital losses upon the surprised
and disappointed potential borrower. One way in which widespread bank
failures affected the economy was by rupturing normal financial channels.
When the Bank of the United States in New York failed in 1930, not only
were there losses by depositors but a fairly large portion of the New York
garment trade was cast adrift without a continuing bank relationship.
Thus in principle we can be cavalier with respect to financial constraint
resulting in loan contraction, but in fact we must recognize that extreme
constraint may cause losses to innocent bystanders. See footnote 9 pp. 309
and 310 in M. Friedman and A. J. Schwartz, Money and Business Cycles.

Purchased liabilities include Federal funds and large certificates of deposits for commercial banks as well as out-of-state deposits for savings and loan associations. Market demand may be volatile with respect to system performance for purchased liabilities, but be stable for service liabilities. A bank's potential ability to finance a position in assets without recourse to extraordinary techniques in times of monetary constraint may depend upon the extent to which its resources are derived from service rather than from purchased liabilities. The potential for recourse either to the discount window or to the sale of assets in some secondary market is related directly to the extent to which purchased liabilities are a source of funds. Thus the cash flow examination will have to consider the likelihood that the behavior of the market for such bank liabilities will lead to large cash flows out of the bank and thus force it to resort to discounting or asset sales.

Any cash flow analysis would need to relate each earning asset - both loans and investments - to the market in which they may be sold or pledged. For each asset the terms upon which financing is available to the position takers or lenders in its market need to be examined. In particular the breadth, depth, and resiliency of a market can be guaranteed only if the central bank or perhaps its chosen instruments stand ready to finance position takers. Thus if new asset classes become important, the examinations procedure might feed back to the central bank the need for the development of new or strengthened secondary markets or additional discount facilities.

For the demand and contingent liabilities of deposit institutions the interesting economic question is the conditions under which the demand or contingent claims will be exercised.

The cash flow to and from an organization because of demand liabilities is a function of at least the terms offered by the institution, the terms available elsewhere, and for certain institutions, national income. Many special variables that reflect the specific contractual terms enter into determining the impact upon   cash flows of market-determined and policy variables. [44/]

The content of cash flow analysis of a financial intermediary can be made more precise by illustrating how the technique would be applied to a specific institution. Let us take, for the sake of simplicity, and also perhaps because of its recent relevance, a savings and loan association. The assets of such an institution will consist almost entirely of long-term fully amortized mortgages. Because of the rapid growth of these institutions the representative portfolio is rather young. This means that the cash flow to the organization on account of its assets is a relatively small percentage of the total liabilities. In addition to such mortgages there will be some cash and Treasury bills - but at most these will be a small percentage of total assets. Thus even allowing for the cash flow which

---

44/ In the Minsky- Bonem simulation experiments, reported in my paper, "Financial Crisis, Financial Systems, and the Performance of the Economy," pp. 365 and 366 - least square regression lines were fitted for new deposits and withdrawals at savings and loan organizations as functions of disposable income. For particular savings and loan organizations similar functions would need to be estimated and such functions would include local economic conditions as well as interest rate variables, rather than just aggregate income data as was true in our rather primitive analysis.

the management can generate by selling assets, the cash flow to the organization during one short period (say 90 days) cannot be more than 5 per cent to 10 per cent of total liabilities.

Ignoring standby and lender of last resort refinancing as a potential supplier of cash, these organizations must at all times offer sufficiently attractive interest rates that no appreciable flight of deposits will occur. However as they cannot discriminate readily among depositors, they must pay all depositors whatever is needed to keep the marginal depositor.

In the summer of 1966, the need arose to raise interest rates on all deposits to prevent the large-scale withdrawals of some deposits. This resulted in a sharp rise in the total cost of deposit funds. At the same time savings banks were locked into young portfolios whose contracts reflect lower interest rates of the past. The cost of money in many cases may be penal, but unlike the classical penal rate case, the penal rate will rule not for a short time but may stretch over many years.

The penal rate of classical banking theory was an expensive way of refinancing a position that ran off in the relatively short span of time: 90 to 180 days. As a result of the short original dating of the contracts, within 6 months almost all of the initial assets of a commercial bank will be repaid, the turnover time for assets is short. New assets will be acquired as old ones are repaid, but only at interest rates that are consistent with the higher cost of money. Thus when the cost of money rises, the relevant question is not just "How long will the interest rates be at this higher level?" but also "How long will it take for almost all assets

in the portfolio to carry rates consistent with the new rate on liabilities?"
If portfolios are heavily weighted with young, fully amortized, long-term
contracts, this turnaround time can be many years. A cash flow examination
procedure would state how long it would take for say 25 per cent, 50 per cent,
and 75 per cent of assets to adjust to new higher--or lower--costs of money.

If interest on liabilities is a cash flow from the organization, a
period in which a net cash flow out is financed by selling assets can occur
when interest rates rise. If interest on liabilities is credited to the
accounts of the depositors, deposit liabilities will rise relative to
assets, and net worth will decrease. In both cases demand commitments to
pay will increase relative to both the contractual cash flow to the unit
due to assets and the ability of management to generate a cash flow by
selling marketable assets.

There is no need to enlarge upon the conditional relations that
are relevant. For example one possible reaction by a deposit institution
to prospective pressures for cash payments is to increase the ratio of cash
and marketable securities to other assets. This means that instead of
feeding cash flows generated by its mortgage portfolios to the now high-
yielding mortgages, a hard pressed savings and loan association will withdraw from the mortgage market and use cash flows to acquire low-yielding
but marketable assets: it prepares its cash and near-cash position to
withstand a deposit drain.

For each of various assumptions as to how units react to a cumulative
cash flow to or cash flow from, a time series of asset and liability positions
can be derived. Presumably in the example given, the cash flow from,

because of withdrawals, can actually be greater than the cash flow to
some periods. Even if such withdrawals do not occur, and even if we
do not value assets at the current--estimated--market price, the growth
of demand liabilities that results from the crediting of the high interest
rate income to deposit accounts will lead to an increase in the ratio of
deposit liabilities to cash flow to the organization. Thus it may become
an ever more difficult problem to retain deposits.

A conditional cash flow examination of individual and classes of
financial institutions would determine the impact upon the institution or
class of institution of various policy-determined conditions.

One proposition favored by nonacademics is that the high cost of
funds forces financial intermediaries into making risky loans that carry a high
contractual interest rate. From the above cash flow example it is possible
for the cost of funds to rise so rapidly, relative to the fixed returns on
the assets, that the organization foresees a liquidity crisis at some stated
date is certain if it follows a conservative policy in the placement of
accruing cash. If it sells its low-yield, fixed-market-price investments,
reduces its cash position, and uses the cash flow on principal, income,
and new deposit accounts to purchase high-yield, high-risk assets, then,
if all turns out well, it avoids a liquidity crisis. That is, whereas the
conservative portfolio policy yields a financial crisis with a probability
of almost one, the more radical portfolio policy yields a finite probability
greater than zero of avoiding the liquidity crisis. In these conditions
the chancy portfolio policy is safer than the risk-free policy.

A conditional cash flow analysis of individual, and classes of, financial institutions will estimate the impact of various alternative policy and market-determined conditions upon the individual institutions and the set of institutions. For example, there may be a limit to tight money - due to the running losses, as illustrated above - that a nonbank financial intermediary - such as the savings and loan associations - can stand. The Federal Reserve System must look beyond the commercial banking system to determine whether, or in what circumstances, its actions are destabilizing.

A unified procedure for examining all financial institutions that focuses on their cash flows will be of help not only to unit managements but also to regulatory authorities. One advantage of this approach is that through the information obtained the distribution of impacts can be estimated. Such an examination procedure should enable us to determine how many units are pushed over or pushed too close to some threshold by some constraining event that, for example, lowers the average return to a financial intermediary.

The development of a cash-flow-oriented bank and other financial institution examination procedure will involve a great deal of experimentation not only with observations on individual banks - the data gathered in examinations - but also with the system attributes that are relevant to determining individual bank behavior. Fortunately the recent interest in banking and bank markets has generated a body of studies that can be used as a starting point for the analysis of the behavior of financial institutions under alternative conditions.

VIII. Regional Aspects of Growth and Financial Instability.

        The reserve base of the banks in a region must be earned, and to keep such reserves the return offered must be competitive. The global reserve base is the result of Federal Reserve policies.[45/] Every change in reserves appears initially as a change in reserves in some particular set of banks. However, even if the Federal Reserve has a policy or program that directs the initial change in reserves toward some region, the ultimate regional distribution depends upon market forces. Any change in the reserve base of the banks within any region will be the result of either an income or an asset transaction with the rest of the country. The monetary system of every region is equivalent to a very strict gold standard, where reserves for a region are the equivalent of gold for a country.

        National economic growth is the result of the growth of the various regions. Some regions grow more rapidly - and some less rapidly - than the economy. The available evidence indicates that the reserve base of the various regions grows at a pace that is consistent with the growth of the region. That is, even if there is a trend in velocity in both the country and the regions, the relative velocity will change but slightly. If there is a rapidly growing region embedded in a slowly growing country - as was true of California during the 1950's - the money supply and the reserve base of the

---

45/   Even if there are changes in the reserve base that are not due to Federal Reserve policy, the total reserve change is the result of Federal Reserve action—or inaction.

rapidly growing region will also grow rapidly. Thus, in the 1950's while demand deposits in the United States were growing slowly, demand deposits in California were growing rapidly.[46]

In the case of California, two identifiable, large, and rapidly growing sources of bank reserves were (1) the excess of Federal Government payments over receipts in the State and (2) the flow of funds to the State to finance home construction. Other sources of reserves undoubtedly exist, but they were not identifiable at the time of the research underlying this section.

During the decade of the 1950's, the financing of housing generated a large flow of funds towards California. It has been estimated that as much as 40 per cent of the total finance for house building in California came from out of the State. This flow of funds into California reflected both the export of mortgages and a rise in out-of-state deposits in California savings and loan associations. About 20 per cent of the deposits in California savings and loan associations were from out-of-state depositors.

A build-up in the stock of mortgages and deposits owned by out-of-state investors means that an increasing reserve drain takes place to meet the commitments as stated in this growing stock of liabilities. That is, without an appropriate offsetting growth in the cash flow from new mortgages, deposits, or other items, the growing stock of outstanding liabilities will tend to generate payments that lower the region's reserve base. Any slowdown in the influx of funds to the region on account of the housing market can lower the growth prospects for commercial banks and for the State's money supply.

46/ See Minsky (ed.), <u>California Banking in a Growing Economy: 1946-1975</u>.

Mortgages, especially the standard fully amortized contract, generate a known, dated series of payments; the only variation in the cash drain from the region due to the stock of mortgages will be due to an inability to make payments, prepayments, or the sale of mortgages. Given that there is some experience on prepayments and sales, it seems clear that the outstanding foreign-owned (out-of-state) mortgages yield a known cash drain from the regions' banks.

The cash flow due to all depositors but especially those from out of State, at California savings and loan associations will depend upon safety and profitability. Deposit insurance eliminates concern or doubt about the safety; thus, the cash flow to California on account of savings and loan deposits depends upon relative interest rates. A variety of rate-sensitive 'hot monies' exist as deposits in these institutions; some of these would be sensitive to small differentials in interest rates. We would expect these potentially hot-money deposits to be the large out-of-state accounts.

Even though all deposits - local and out of State - should be equally sensitive to rate differentials, the convenience factor may dominate in the case of local, mostly passbook deposits. A rapidly growing region must maintain a rate structure that attracts funds and that retains previously acquired out-of-state deposit funds. Thus, California savings and loan associations must keep a favorable interest rate premium, even if the demand for housing financing is slack. Defensive rate competition is based upon the unit's liability structure. Note that if the national cost of money is high, the supply price of finance from these institutions will

remain consistent with this cost of money, even though local demands for
financing may be slack.

One impact of monetary constraint in a euphoric economy is that a
rise has taken place in other market interest rates relative to the rate
on California savings and loan shares (deposits). The observation that the
California mortgage market exhibited signs of disorderly conditions in mid-
1966 needs no documentation. Due to rate competition, these deposits have
stopped increasing. Even if there is a net increase in deposits (at a
slower rate) the net increase may be compounded of a decrease in foreign
(out-of-state) deposits that is more than offset by rise in domestic (in-
state) deposits.

During recent periods of monetary constraint, the housing-related
financial markets have tended to generate a decrease in California's reserve
base. If all else remains the same this means that either monetary velocity
in California must increase relative to that of other geographical sectors,
or the rate of growth of income must decrease.

There is nothing sacred about the favored growth experience of
California, nor is there any reason why the national authorities should
operate to keep California growing more rapidly than the country as a whole.
However, tight money will be particularly hard on California home-building,
mortgage financing institutions, and commercial banks. This will be compounded
if a rate ceiling is adopted to prevent competition for deposits. Non-
constrained market instruments are substitutes for saving and loan liabilities,
and a potential expansion of the retailing of such market instruments is a
threat to deposit institutions.

A decline, or a slowdown, in the growth of commercial bank reserves in a rapidly growing region will lead to a decline in locally available credit through commercial banks. California banks are traditionally light on secondary reserve assets. The opportunity to sustain loan growth by decreasing investments is minimal.

Monetary constraint, after a period of rapid growth--especially if such constant is a reaction to a spread of euphoria from a previously rapidly growing region to the country as a whole--will put serious pressures upon the banks and other financial institutions of the previously rapidly growing region. The regional concentration of financial duress may trigger a more general spread of distress than if the same total financial tightness were more evenly distributed geographically.

The practioneer of monetary policy must be aware that there are differential regional pressures due to monetary constraint and that contagion phenomena within a region may be one way in which financial instability may be initiated.

IX.   Central Banking.

The modern central bank has at least two facets: a part of the
stabilization and growth-inducing apparatus of Government and the lender
of last resort to all or part of the financial system.   These two functions
can conflict.

For the United States, central bank functions are decentralized
among the Federal Reserve System, the various deposit insurance and saving
intermediary regulatory bodies, and the Treasury.   The decentralization
of central banking functions and responsibilities makes it possible for
"buck passing" to occur.   One result of this decentralization, along with
the fact of usage and market evolution, is that there exists a perennial
problem of defining the scope and functions of the various arms of the
central bank.   The behavior of the various agencies in mid-1966 indicates
that <u>ad hoc</u> arrangements among the various agencies can serve as the <u>de
facto</u> central bank.   However, even though central banking functions are
distributed among a number of organizations, the fact that the Federal
Reserve System is first among the set should not be obscured.   The Federal
Reserve System may have to make markets in the assets or liabilities of
these other institutions if they are to be able to carry out their assigned
sub-routines.

The Federal Reserve System undertook, when the peg was removed
from the Government bond market, to maintain orderly conditions in this
market.   Maintaining orderly conditions in a key asset market is an
extension of the lender-of-last-resort functions in that it is a preventive
lender of last resort.   "If we allow the now disorderly conditions

to persist, we will in fact have to be a lender of last resort" is the underlying rationalization behind such action. Maintaining orderly conditions
in some markets serves to protect position takers in the instrument traded
in these markets. This protection of position takers may be a necessary
ingredient for the development of efficient financial markets.

The stabilizer and lender-of-last-resort functions are most
directly in conflict as a result of such efforts to maintain orderly
conditions. If constraining action, undertaken to stabilize income, threatens
the solvency of financial institutions, the central bank will be forced
to back away from the policy of constraint.

If a financial crisis occurs, the central bank must abandon
any policy of constraint. Presumably the central bank should intervene
before a collapse of market asset values that will lead to a serious
depression. However, if it acts too soon and is too effective, there will
be no appreciable pause to the expansion that made the policy of constraint
necessary.

I have discussed already one way in which tight money can cause
financial instability; that is, asset holders are forced into risky portfolio decisions that are locked into assets bearing terms born in times of
greater ease. In addition the very rise in interest rates, which measures
tight money, induces substitutions in portfolios that makes more likely
financial instability hus intervention on grounds of lender of last
resort and responsibilities for maintaining of orderly conditions become
more likely during such periods.

In exuberant economic conditions central banking has to determine just how disorderly markets can become, once distress appears, before the lender-of-last-resort functions take over and dominate its actions. Perhaps the optimal way to handle a euphoric economy is to allow a crisis to develop--so that the portfolios acceptable under euphoric conditions are found to be dangerous--but to act before any severe losses in market values such as are associated with an actual crisis take place. If monetary conditions are eased too soon, then no substantial unlayering of balance sheets will be induced, and the total effect of monetary actions might very well be to reinforce the euphoric expansion. If conditions are eased after a crisis actually occurs - so that desired portfolios have been revised to allow for more protection - but the effective exercise of lender-of-last-resort functions prevents too great a fall in asset prices, then the euphoria will be terminated and a more sustainable relation, in terms of investment demand, between the capital stock and desired capital will be established. If the lender-of-last-resort functions are exercised too late and too little, then the decline in asset prices will lead to a stagnation of investment and a deeper and more protracted recession. Given that the error of easing too soon only delays the problem of constraining an euphoric situation, it may be that the best choice for monetary policy really involves preventing those more severe losses in asset prices that lead to deep depressions, rather than preventing any disorderly or near-crisis conditions. If capitalism reacts to past success by trying to explode, it may be that the only effective way to stabilize the system, short of direct investment controls, is to allow minor financial crises to occur from time to time.

82.

Note that the above is independent of the mix of policies. If,
as seems evident, the tight money of 1965-66 was due more to a rapid rise
in the demand for money than to a decline in the rate of growth of the
supply of money, a greater monetary ease combined with fiscal constraint would
not have done the job. If we accept that a major expansionary element over
this period was the investment boom and that the expenditures attributable
to Vietnam only affected the degree, not the kind, of development, then an
increased availability of finance would have resulted in increased investment
and nominal income. A changed policy mix would have constituted further
evidence of a new era. Of course, the fiscal constraint could have been
severe enough to cause such a large decline in private incomes that existing
commitments to make payments could not be met. A financial crisis or a close
equivalent may be induced by too severe an application of fiscal constraint
as well as by undue monetary constraint.

Within the Federal Reserve System, from the perspective of the maintenance of financial stability or at least the minimization of the impact
upon income and employment of instability, a reversal may be in order of
the trend that has led to the attenuation of the discount window. If
secondary markets are to grow as a way of generating both liquidity while
the system is functioning normally and protection while the system is in
difficulties, then the dealers in these markets will need access to
guaranteed refinancing. The only truly believable guaranty is that of
the central bank.

However, a central bank's promise to intervene to maintain orderly
conditions in some market will be credible only if the central bank is

operating already in that market. If the central bank is not operating in the market, then it will not have working relations with market participants and it will not be receiving first-hand and continuous information as to conditions in the market; no regular channels that feed information about market conditions will exist as now exist for the Government bond market. Thus the Federal Reserve will need to be a normal functioning supplier of funds to the secondary markets it desires to promote.

At present, only a small portion of the total reserve base of banks is due to discounting at the Federal Reserve System. Discounting can serve three functions - a temporary offset to money market pressures, a steady source of reserves, and the route for emergency stabilization of prices. In order to set the ground for the Federal Reserve System to function effectively in the event of a crisis that requires a lender of last resort, the Federal Reserve normally should be "dealing" or "discounting" in a wide variety of asset markets. One way to do this is to encourage the emergence of dealer secondary markets in various assets and to have the Federal Reserve supply some of the regular financing of the dealers. It might be that a much higher percentage of the bank cash assets than at present should be the result of discounting, but the discounting should be by market organizations rather than banks.

Monetary and fiscal constraint may not be enough once the Keynesian lessons have been learned. The monetary - fiscal steering wheel had assumed a mechanistic determination of decisions that in reality center around uncertainty; and the system doing well may so affect uncertainty that an arsenal of stabilization weapons that includes larger rationing elements may be necessary.

Let us assume the present arsenal of policy weapons and objectives. The policy objectives will be taken to mean that the high-level stagnation of the 1952-60 period does not constitute an acceptable performance. Under these conditions, the lender-of-last-resort obligations of the Federal Reserve, redefined as allowing local or minor financial crises to occur while sustaining over-all asset prices against large declines, become the most important dimension of Federal Reserve policy. The lender-of-last-resort responsibilities become also the arena **where** human error may play a significant role in determining the actual outcome of economic situations.

It is only in a taut, euphoric, and potentially explosive economy that there is much scope for error by the central bank. The importance attached to human error under these circumstances is due to a system characteristic - the tendency to explode - rather than to the failings of the Board of Governors.

BIBLIOGRAPHY

Ackley, G. Macroeconomic Theory. New York: Macmillan, 1961.

Arrow, K. J. Aspects of the Theory of Risk Bearing. Yrjo Jahnsson lectures.
Helsinki: Yrjo Jahnssonin Säätio, 1965.

_____. "Uncertainty and the Welfare Economics of Medical Care,"
American Economic Review, December 1963.

Clower, R. W. "An Investigation into the Dynamics of Investment," American
Economic Review, March 1954.

Economic Report of the President. Washington D. C.: U. S. Government Printing
Office, 1969.

Fellner, W. "Average-Cost Pricing and the Theory of Uncertainty," Journal
of Political Economy, June 1948.

_____. "Monetary Policies and Hoarding in Periods of Stagnation,"
Journal of Political Economy, June 1943.

Fisher, I. "The Debt-Deflation Theory of Great Depressions," Econometrica,
October 1933.

Friedman, M. "The Demand for Money: Some Theoretical and Empirical Results,"
Journal of Political Economy, August 1959.

Friedman, M., and Schwartz, A. J. A Monetary History of the United States
1867-1960. Study by the National Bureau of Economic Research,
N.Y. N.J.: Princeton University Press, 1963.

_____. "Money and Business Cycles," Review of
of Economics and Statistics, Supplement, February 1963.

Galbraith, J. K. The Affluent Society. Boston: Houghton Mifflin, 1958.

Greenberg, E. "A Stock-Adjustment Investment Model," Econometrica,
July 1964.

Gurley, J. G., and Shaw, E. Money in a Theory of Finance. Washington D.C.:
Brookings Institution, 1960.

Hicks, J. R. "Mr. Keynes and the 'Classics,' A Suggested Interpretation,"
Econometrica, April 1937.

Johnson, H. G. "The 'General Theory' after Twenty-five Years," American
Economic Review, papers and proceedings, May 1961.

Kalecki, M. "The Principle of Increasing Risk," Economica, November 1937.

Keynes, J. M. "The General Theory of Employment," Quarterly Journal of
Economics, February 1937.

Minsky, H. P. "Central Banking and Money Market Changes," Quarterly Journal
of Economics, May 1957.

Minsky, H. P. (ed.) California Banking in a Growing Economy: 1946-1975,
Berkeley, California: University of California, Institute
of Business and Economic Research, 1965.

_____. "Comment on Friedman and Schwartz's Money and Business Cycles,"
Review of Economics and Statistics, Supplement, February 1963.

_____. "Financial Crisis, Financial Systems, and the Performance of
the Economy," in Private Capital Markets. Prepared for the
Commission on Money and Credit, N.Y. Englewood Cliffs, N.J.:
Prentice-Hall, Inc., 1964.

_____. "Financial Intermediation in the Money and Capital Markets,"
in Pontecorvo, G., Shay, R. P., and Hart, A. G. Issues in
Banking and Monetary Analysis. New York: Holt, Rinehart and
Winston, Inc., 1967.

_____. "A Linear Model of Cyclical Growth," <u>Review of Economics and</u> <u>Statistics</u>, May 1959; also in Gordon, R. A., and Klein, L. R., A.E.A. Readings in Business Cycles, ol. 10. Homewood, Ill.: Richard D. Irwin, Inc., 1965.

Ozga, S. A. Expectations in Economic Theory. Chicago: Aldine Publishing Co., 1965.

Tobin, J. <u>The Intellectual Revolution in U.S. Economic Policy Making</u>. Noel Buxton lecture. Essex, Great Britain: The University of Essex, 1966.

"Liquidity Preference as Behavior Towards Risk," <u>Review of Economic</u> <u>Studies</u>, February 1958.

Turvey, R. "Does the Rate of Interest Rule the Roost," in Hahn, F. H., and Brechling, F.P.R. (eds.) <u>The Theory of Interest Rates</u>. New York: St. Martin's Press, 1965.

Viner, J. "Mr. Keynes on the Causes of Unemployment," <u>Quarterly Journal of</u> <u>Economics</u>, November 1936.

Witte, J. G., Jr. "The Microfoundations of the Social Investment Function," <u>Journal of Political Economy</u>, October 1963.

CPSIA information can be obtained
at www.ICGtesting.com
Printed in the USA
LVHW080538170519
618209LV00009B/200/P